TIME

# Dealing with Doubt

David J. Randall

DayOne

British Library Cataloguing in Publication Data available
Published by Day One Publications
Ryelands Road, Leominster, HR6 8NZ
Telephone 01568 613 740 FAX 01568 611 473
email—sales@dayone.co.uk
web site—www.dayone.co.uk

Cover design by Kathryn Chedgzoy
Printed by 4edge

# Endorsements

*'I have my doubts' is a common phrase in my native Scotland. It reflects a careful and realistic rather than a cynical approach. Sometimes Christians are faced with doubts of another kind—the fears and questions which come from our culture, our own sinful hearts and above all the father of lies. How do we deal with these? This short book is a helpful biblical, practical analysis of doubt and how we deal with it in different circumstances. Excellent.*

**Rev David Robertson, Minister & Evangelist—Hamilton Presbyterian church, Newcastle, NSW, Australia; author of The Dawkins Letters and Magnificent Obsession.**

*'This book, written with warmth, sensitivity, and sound Biblical application, will be a huge help to many ordinary Christians as they struggle with the perplexing questions that challenge their faith.'*

**Rev Iver Martin, Principal, Edinburgh Theological Seminary**

*Doubt of various sorts—about God's goodness, power, truth, and many other things—is a common experience for those who are Christians and a common objection for those who are not. David Randall has written a book which looks doubts squarely in the face. He shows us that many in the pages of the Bible walked these paths before us, and found the God of the Bible fully answered them with the wonder of his nature and the power of his Word. Randall brings us face to face not simply with arguments to deal with doubt but with a glorious and gracious God who overwhelms it.*

**Rev Dr Matthew Roberts, Minister—Trinity Church, York; author of Pride—Identity & the Worship of Self.**

*Doubts on faith's journey are excruciating—or at least they probably should be. The questions dealt with here could not be more profound, nor the outcome more serious. What matters most then on the journey is travelling companions and fixed points to steer by. Randall deals, in a series of tightly focused scriptural case studies, with almost every category of doubt, from the stable position of someone who has* charted a course by the certainties of God's Word and his self-revelation as Truth in Christ alone. Read this as a rich repository of triangulation points on that journey and be encouraged.

**Dr John Ellis, Consultant Ophthalmologist, Ninewells Hospital, Dundee**

David's book is pastoral, biblical and conversant with the challenges we face when expressing our faith in and to a sceptical world. He acknowledges the challenge, giving the reader the necessary equipment to carry on the journey of faith. Whether you are facing doubt yourself or need a clear biblical guide about the subject, Dealing with Doubt *will be an excellent read.*

**Rev Alberto de Paula, Minister – Broughty Ferry Presbyterian Church**

Most Christians face times when they feel like the man in Mark 9 who said, 'I believe; help my unbelief.' In this book, David Randall serves as a wise pastor to all who struggle with doubt by pinpointing its most common causes and offering biblical insight as to how it is overcome. An aid for pastors in shepherding their flocks; a comfort to struggling pilgrims on the way and a help to the church at large as she reaches out to an unbelieving world, this book contains a rich store of wisdom from one who has ministered to God's people for more than fifty years.

**Rev Paul Gibson, Minister – Knox Church Perth, a congregation of the Free Church of Scotland**

David has taken a real and big subject and helpfully addressed 'doubt' from many angles. He unpacks incidents and characters in the Bible through the lens of questions and experiences that often give rise to doubts in our minds about God and His character. I believe this book will help many to honestly and courageously face questions and doubts about the Christian faith without being afraid. Even in this area, God has placed, in the Bible, people from whom we can learn. This is a wide-ranging exploration that will 'help our unbelief'.

**Elaine Duncan, CEO, Scottish Bible Society**

# Contents

# Foreword

I had the wonderful privilege of being raised in a Christian home. Some of my earliest memories are of the Baptist Church I attended as a child (I think my parents' motto was: 'You don't need to be a Baptist to go to heaven, but why take the risk?'). I learned tremendous amounts about Jesus from my church leaders, from my parents and from friends. Then, aged about twelve, on a dark and stormy night at a youth camp on the cliffs above Hastings on England's south coast, I made my own personal commitment to follow Christ.

As I grew into my teenage years, I soon discovered the first serious challenges to my young faith. We lived in a very multicultural part of London and the school I attended was stuffed full of kids from other religions—indeed some of my best friends were Muslims, Hindu, Jewish and, in one case, a kid who self-identified as a Jedi (he was a force to be reckoned with). I began asking questions like, 'If Christianity is uniquely true, what does that mean for my friends who believe as passionately as I do but differently?' Similarly, questions about science, or the historicity of the Bible, arose naturally from my studies and I wrestled with those too.

Further doubts came along when, in my early twenties, I experienced a severe period of depression and, for over a year, life seemed incredibly bleak and pointless. An excellent GP and wonderful pastoral support at church helped me back to good mental health but, nevertheless, depression brought home the problem of suffering in a very real and highly personal way.

Whether the cause was tough questions or personal suffering, whenever the doubts came, I remember worrying that I was a second-rate Christian. Weren't Christians supposed to march onward victoriously, wearing the belt of truth, the helmet of salvation, and the other armour of God listed in Ephesians 6? Meanwhile my own spiritual attire seemed more akin to the dungarees of doubt and the underpants of uncertainty. Just like real men don't eat pineapple quiche or do mime on a Wednesday, so I figured that real Christians don't doubt.

In the end, there were three things that brought me through all this. Firstly, there were the older, wiser Christian friends and family who listened patiently to my doubts and questions and helped me address and tackle them. Secondly, there are the many stories in the Bible of heroes of faith who doubted (think of some of David's very honest psalms, or John the Baptist's anxiety in prison, or Thomas' famous doubting moment). And thirdly, there was the realization that I was not alone—that many Christians experience times of doubt, including some of the giants of faith I admired. For example, William Wilberforce, the abolitionist and social reformer, whose faith led him to transform society, was a huge hero of mine. Yet right at the end of a life well lived for the Lord, he wavered. On his death bed, his health failing, Wilberforce whispered, 'I am in a very distressed state.' His son, Henry, replied, 'Yes, but you have your feet on the Rock.' Wilberforce's final words were, 'I do not venture to speak so positively. But I hope I have.' It's encouraging to know that, when we doubt, we are not alone in the experience.

Looking back, I also realize that some of my doubts as a young Christian were not helped because I had some wrong ideas about faith. I was not alone in this either: faith is a very commonly misunderstood word. It's often taken (outside the church) to mean 'believing things for which you don't have any evidence', or (inside the church) 'grit your teeth, recite the creeds, and don't ask too many questions'.

When I first discovered that the biblical word *faith* really means 'placing one's trust in', it was transformative. For not merely do we have remarkably good evidence to trust Jesus; the other thing about trust is that it doesn't matter how strong or weak your trust is, what matters is in whom you trust. The strength of our faith may ebb and flow but Jesus is entirely dependable—the same yesterday, today and forever.

I am grateful that God brought me through those struggles of the early years of my faith—and my experiences give me tremendous compassion for those who wrestle with doubt today.

I now answer tough questions for a living and I love hearing the questions of those who are seeking faith, exploring faith, or growing in their faith. I passionately believe that the Church should be a place which *welcomes* questions, just as Jesus Himself did. If we tackle people's honest questions, that helps overcome roadblocks to faith and also helps prevent those questions tripping up Christians.

In my almost forty years of following Jesus, I have learned—and continue daily to learn—that following Jesus is a journey. Sometimes we get in trouble because we expect that on day one (or day ten, or day four hundred and twenty-one) all of our struggles will be over and it will be easy. That naïve assumption is a guaranteed way to disappointment or even disaster. Challenges will come. The doubts will occasionally rear their heads. The underpants of uncertainty will occasionally fall out of the wardrobe. But we don't need to be afraid of any of this because in the words of Richard Bewes' hymn (based on Psalm 46):[1]

> God is our strength and refuge,
> our present help in trouble,
> and we therefore will not fear,
> though the earth should change!
> Though mountains shake and tremble,
> though swirling floods are raging,
> God the Lord of hosts is with us evermore!

Doubt is not unusual and we can't prevent the fears, anxiety, or questions that will emerge as, like Christian in *The Pilgrim's Progress*, we tramp, tramp, tramp our way towards the Celestial City. We can't stop the doubts coming. But we can decide what to do when they come. And books like David's are incredibly helpful in encouraging us when they do. Not least, he's done a wonderful job showing how many of the giants of the Bible wrestled with doubts and uncertainties, but that God both led them through and used them, doubts and all.

My hope and my prayer is that this short book will inspire and challenge you, comfort and equip you, whether you're dealing with doubt yourself, or helping to support others who are. And if you personally are wrestling with doubt, remember the promise of Psalm 23: that no matter how deep or dark the valley of your doubts,

God is walking with you through them—both leading you like the Good Shepherd He is, but also with His goodness and mercy bringing up the rear.[2] You are hemmed in by the love of a God who, in His love and kindness, has not left us to face the difficulties of the world alone. May this book encourage you to follow Him faithfully no matter what life throws at you.

Dr Andy Bannister,

Director, Solas,

November 2023

### NOTES

1 Bewes, Richard, 'God is our Strength and Refuge', (Jubilate Hymns Ltd, sub to Hope Publishing, 1982). As a child, I loved the fact that the tune to this hymn was *The Dam Busters March* from the famous war movie. A friend and I once got in trouble in church one Sunday for making what we thought were suitable aeroplane noises during the singing of it.

2 This point is made beautifully by F. W. Boreham in his little book, *In Pastures Green: A Ramble through the Twenty-Third Psalm* (London: The Epworth Press, 1954).

# Preface

Dear Pastor,

I'm writing to ask for your help. As you know I stood up in church some time ago and professed my faith and took my vows. I am happy to be part of the church family, but recently I have to confess that I've been having doubts about some aspects of Christianity. I assume that real Christians shouldn't have such doubts, so I'm confused.

As I attend the services, it seems as if everybody else is blissfully confident in their faith, and your sermons always come across with conviction. Sometimes I'm not sure that I really belong there. I wasn't even sure that I should tell you about all of this but on the other hand, I want to be honest and I don't want to pretend that everything is plain and straightforward when it isn't.

So, I'd like to ask: am I the only one to experience such doubts about God and the Bible? Have you ever had doubts? Should I stop attending church until my doubts are cleared up? And do my doubts actually prove that I was never a true Christian in the first place?

I'm sorry to be troubling you with all of this, and I hope you won't be too disappointed in me when you receive this message, but I'd be glad of any help you can give.

Yours sincerely,

Chris

Dear Chris,

Thanks for your email and let me say at the start that I am not at all disappointed in you. In fact, I'm pleased that you have felt able to write as you did. It's good to bring such things out into the open rather than allowing them to fester away in your mind and heart.

I was delighted when you attended the membership course and then said you were ready to make a public profession of your faith. I know that your parents and grandparents were also very happy that you had committed yourself to the Lord and His family here.

However, in response to your questions, I want to assure you that it's normal to have fluctuations in feelings and that times of doubt don't prove your profession of faith was empty. No doubt some people have made false professions of faith but, from our previous conversations, I'm sure that your commitment is real. Few Christians could say that they've never had any doubts at all and one of the striking things about the Bible is that it honestly faces up to such doubts. In the pages that follow, I want to consider how these doubts were handled, and I hope this will be helpful.

In the meantime—to respond to another of your questions— please don't cut yourself off from the church family. I hope you'll continue to share in the worship and fellowship of the church. You wrote about other people in church seeming very confident and untroubled, but I know that many people have come through trying times, as I have also.

My hope and prayer for you is that, as you face up to your questions, you will be helped by One who said, 'I am … the truth' (John 14:6). May you find your doubts decreasing and your faith growing stronger as the days go by. Please let me know what you make of the chapters that follow.

Thanks for communicating your thoughts and may the Lord Himself guide us all into a stronger and stronger faith.

Yours,

David

# Introduction

The Bible is a book of faith and Christianity is, from the human angle, about having faith. The Bible's goal is to make us wise for salvation through faith in Christ Jesus (2 Timothy 3:15), and it tells the stories of many people who exercised such faith.

Luke says that he wrote for someone called Theophilus, in order that he might have certainty concerning the things he had been taught (Luke 1:4). Maybe Theophilus had had doubts and Luke wanted to help him.

And John tells us that he wrote his Gospel so that its readers 'may believe that Jesus is the Christ, the Son of God, and that by believing [we] ... may have life in his name' (John 20:31). Whether John was talking about bringing people to faith in the first place or encouraging them to hold firm in that faith (or perhaps both), this really is the thrust of the whole Bible.

The Bible is a book of faith and, despite much questioning in recent generations—whether from scholarly sceptics or popular songwriters with their assertion about the content of the Bible that, 'it ain't necessarily so'[1]—it has led millions of people to faith, confirmed them in that faith and inspired them to be faithful to the God revealed in its pages.

However, all of that does not mean that it is always *easy* to have such faith or to persevere in it. The famous C. S. Lewis, who was one of the twentieth-century's best-known advocates for the truth of

Christianity, wrote candidly about his periodic times of doubt: 'Now that I am a Christian, I do have moods in which the whole thing looks very improbable: but, when I was an atheist, I had moods in which Christianity looked terribly probable.'[2]

Lewis' books have convinced many people of the truth of Christianity and also confirmed many believers who may have wavered in their faith and wondered at times whether they had been mistaken when they decided to accept Christ. It is interesting to find that such a renowned apologist[3] also had times when doubts crept into his mind. The passage from which Lewis' words are taken is about holding by your faith in spite of changing moods: 'Unless you teach your moods "where they get off", you can never be either a sound Christian or even a sound atheist, but just a creature dithering to and from, with its beliefs really dependent on the weather and the state of its digestion.'[4]

It works both ways. What if, now that you are a Christian, you have these 'moods in which the whole thing looks very improbable'. That is what this book is about.

And it is not only 'moods' that affect us. There are many things that 'come up' which seem to call our faith in question. In the West, we live in a society in which many (especially among the opinion formers) have turned their backs on Christianity; 'religion' may be brought out for formal occasions, but so far as actual living is concerned, they go along with the assumption that it can be left behind with Santa Claus and the tooth fairy.

This becomes very obvious in the area of morality, and particularly in the context of the contemporary sexual revolution which has rejected biblical values and sometimes treated them with hatred and contempt. Believers may sometimes be tempted to wonder whether we can any longer cling to the old ways. We are so out-of-step that we are made to wonder if it could be the believing *Johnny* who is out of step and not the rest of the regiment. Should we just give up and go with the flow?

The question may become very personal. It may be, for instance, a nephew who has announced that he has 'changed gender' or a niece who has invited you to her same sex 'marriage' ceremony. And we may be tempted to wonder whether we really are right after all, and whether we can 'hold out' against societal trends.

One writer has commented on the alarming views of certain philosophers about the need to 'protect' children from Christian parents: 'The strategy is not to argue with religious views or to prove them wrong. Rather, it is to subject them to such scorn that they are pushed outside the bounds of acceptable debate.'[5] So much for reasoned argument! I trust that readers of this book, including those with doubts (or even unbelievers) would want a better foundation than that.

Another kind of pressure comes from the widespread notion that science has trumped religion. Even friends who have never really looked into the issues, have simply accepted the commonly assumed view that there is no place for faith in a science-based world, and again the niggling question may insinuate itself into our minds. Is the Bible reliable? Can we hold to it with integrity and in the face of widespread unbelief?

Or it may be that your friend has been struck by cancer and you are challenged about whether it is credible to believe in God when there is so much pain and suffering in the world. I think of my father's cousin, a fit young man who loved tennis and other activities, struck down by rheumatoid arthritis that crippled him and caused great pain and increasing disability for many years. Then there is the large-scale matter of tsunamis and tornadoes and famine.

Others will point to the poor record of professing Christians in the past, when fighting and war have caused unimaginable amounts of pain and suffering, and at the individual level we confront the fact that Betty who is 'supposed to be a Christian' has a fearsome tongue or Jimmy, who attends church, is known to cheat and lie.

So many things may 'come up' to challenge us and cause some people to wonder about the faith they have previously held, whether they were brought up to believe or came to faith later in life.

## Bible doubters

How are we to deal with doubt? This book draws out the fact that the Bible itself includes the stories of people who struggled with issues related to faith. It is one of the impressive things about the Bible. It may go against the assumption of many people that the Bible is a sunshine-all-the-way book about life in an idealized fantasy world, with simple people exercising simple faith in some kind of Never-Never-Land.

The truth is that the same book, that is so unstinting in its message about the God who is worthy of our trust and our praise, is also very honest about the struggles, questions and doubts of many of its leading human characters. The very fact that the Bible is not about such a sanitized world where everything is sweetness and light, means that it is helpful in relation to the questions and doubts that may suggest themselves to our minds also. Hebrews 2:18 says of Jesus, 'Because he himself has suffered when tempted, he is able to help those who are being tempted'—similarly we can say that because the Bible faces up to doubts and questions, it is able to help us.

Every Easter (and at other times too) people in church gatherings sing, 'No more we doubt Thee, glorious Prince of life,' from the inspiring hymn, 'Thine be the glory'. It is a fine sentiment—no more doubts—and the message of Easter is indeed a great antidote to doubt. But it is not that all questions have been answered and all doubts quelled once and for all. The Easter faith of Christianity, even when there are issues that puzzle us, holds to the central and cardinal truths of the gospel, especially in light of the hymn's 'Lo! Jesus meets us, risen from the tomb; lovingly He greets us, scatters fear and gloom.'

Faith also tells us that a day will come when our questions will be answered; things presently seen through a glass darkly (1 Corinthians 13:12[6]) will be as clear as day—a time anticipated by the hymn:

> I'll bless the hand that guided,
> I'll bless the heart that planned,
> When throned where glory dwelleth
> In Immanuel's land.[7]

And in the meantime, 'These unanswered questions are not incompatible with unshaken faith in the triune God and in Jesus Christ, the incarnate Son. The questions are often perplexing. But they are more often the questions of adoring wonder rather than the questions of painful perplexity. So, there should be no surprise if faith should be quite consonant with unresolved questions and difficulties.'[8]

One writer made the point in what he calls a teachable moment with his own daughter. She was working on a jigsaw puzzle and he said, 'Sophia, I wonder what the picture is.' She responded confidently, 'It's Cinderella.' Her Dad pointed out that she did not yet have all the pieces in place, at which Sophia merely tilted her head and said, 'Dad, it's Cinderella!' She went on say that she was sure it was Cinderella 'because I have enough pieces in place'. Her Dad commented, 'My daughter had stumbled on something significant about this broken world…we can know the truth without knowing everything.'[9]

The eleventh chapter of Hebrews gives a list of people who acted 'by faith"—the phrase is found eighteen times in the chapter (along with several other 'faith' references). The passage has been described as a roll call of heroes of faith—people like Abraham and Moses, for example. And, after saying that there was not time to tell all the stories that could be told, the writer went on: 'Therefore, since we are surrounded by so great a cloud of witnesses, let us also lay aside every weight, and sin which clings so closely, and let us run with endurance the race that is set before us, looking to Jesus, the founder and perfecter of our faith' (Hebrews 12:1–2).

But such faith was not a bland or easy thing. One of the examples given (verse 22) is Joseph, whose faith was severely tested. He was victimized by his brothers, sold into slavery, falsely accused of sexual assault and unfairly imprisoned. But, after his release and reconciliation with his family, he gave expression to a faith that had sustained him through thick and thin. He said to the brothers who had mistreated him, 'You meant evil against me, but God meant it for good, to bring it about that many people should be kept alive, as they are today' (Genesis 50:20).

The Bible is a book that calls us to have such faith in the providence, power and love of God and in the gospel message that is its heart and soul, and it is hoped that this little book about times when Bible characters had their doubts will be helpful—not in the sense of helping us too to be doubters; that would be the most spectacular of own goals! Its purpose rather is to encourage faith. May the Bible's honest record of such doubters, and how their doubts were overcome, help to consolidate the faith of believers and encourage faith in the hearts of any unbelievers who read these words, so that we share the sentiment of the hymn:

When doubts and fears arise,

> Teach me Thy way!
> When storms o'erspread the skies,
> Teach me Thy way!
> Shine through the cloud and rain,
> Through sorrow, toil, and pain;
> Make Thou my pathway plain:
> Teach me Thy way.[10]

## Occasions of doubt

We will be looking at doubt occasioned by many and varied circumstances but all in the context of the Bible's central testimony to the person and work of Jesus Christ. If the theory is correct, which sees Mark's gospel as the first of the four Gospels to be written, then the first words we hear from the lips of Jesus (apart from His

boyhood words about being found in his Father's house—Luke 2:49)
are a call to faith: 'Jesus came into Galilee, proclaiming the gospel
of God, and saying, "The time is fulfilled, and the kingdom of God is
at hand; repent and believe in the gospel"' (Mark 1:14–15).

C. S. Lewis wrote about a time when he had come to believe that
there is such a Person as God, but he expressed his hesitations in a
letter:

> I think the trouble with me is lack of faith. I have no rational ground
> for going back on the arguments that convinced me of God's
> existence; but the irrational deadweight of my old sceptical habits,
> and the spirit of this age, and the cares of the day, steal away all my
> lively feeling of the truth; and often when I pray, I wonder if I am not
> posting letters to a non-existent address.[11]

It is an image that evokes a painful memory for me. I was driving
my first car (a red mini) and had stopped for a right turn when a
lorry scraped along the side of my pride and joy. At first, I thought
the driver was not going to stop but I looked in the mirror and saw
that he had stopped some way along the road (too far away to read
the number plate). Back he came to exchange names, etc. In my
innocence I trusted the driver, and I can still remember the address
which he said was the head office of his employers. He assured me
that they would sort things out. Next day when I looked for it—
you've guessed—there was no such address! I had been 'had' and it
was a hard lesson to learn.

Lewis wondered if praying is like 'posting letters to a non-existent
address' but, of course, he came to an increasing belief that that
address is the most real of all.

The famous Martin Luther said, 'The art of doubting is easy, for it is an ability that is born with us.'[12] It is also true that there are particular features of contemporary life that can be occasions of doubt for some people, such as:

- the fact that we cannot answer all the questions that people ask, and even the frustration of finding that unbelievers can put their finger on questions which flummox us, rather than asking the many other questions that we could have answered!
- the very fact that we do not understand everything about God, faith and the Bible. God has revealed the things we *need* to know (Deuteronomy 29:29) but there are so many things that are still beyond our understanding.
- the imperfections of the church and of Christians. Christians sometimes feel 'let down' by the faults and backslidings of people they had admired and, even knowing that all Christians are 'jars of clay' (2 Corinthians 4:7) and that we should look to Christ and not His followers, such failures, especially when made public for all to see, can cause doubts to arise in some minds.
- misunderstanding of the nature and purpose of trials. God allows difficult times to come 'so that the tested genuineness of your faith' (1 Peter 1:7) may bring glory to Christ, but it is possible to misinterpret such testing experiences and think that God must be against us.
- the trials that come to other people can raise questions too, such as the fearsome sufferings of Job which led his wife to say he should just give in and curse God (Job 2:9).

- the activity of the enemy, the devil, whose activities, as seen in the early chapters of Acts, were summarized by John Stott as persecution, corruption and distraction[13]: the direct attack of persecution (e.g., Acts 4:3), corruption within the church (e.g., Acts 5:1–4) and concentration on non-central matters (e.g., Acts 6:2).
- and, of course, the fact that the social tide is running against us in western culture. We live in a time of widespread scepticism and increasingly virulent attacks on Christianity. Many people find that it is not easy to hold on to Christian faith when voices all around them are simply taking it for granted that 'religion' has had its day, that it is no longer to be tolerated as a benign influence and even that it is dangerous and destructive. Religions tend to be lumped together in such a way, as people assume that we have grown out of earlier primitive ideas and know better nowadays than to believe in God or 'the gods'.

Sometimes this results in an undeferential belligerence against faith[14], and in other cases the simple assumption that we do not go in for that kind of thing any longer. When I was chairman of the Solas Board, I edited a book entitled, *Why We (Still) Believe*,[15] and the publisher's back cover blurb said, 'The West has become permeated with a culture that doesn't "do" God. Many people assert that we have progressed, while Christians are still clinging to out-dated ideas.'

I was interested to see the comment in one review of the book: 'My Year 9 English teacher told me that words in brackets will often communicate the greatest meaning.'[16] So it is with the book's title;

it gives reasons for holding to the revealed truths of Christianity *still*—that is, despite all the attacks and assumptions of those who would relegate the Bible to the shelf for items of historical interest.

Actually, we are not the first generation to face such issues. The nineteenth-century anthropologist, Max Muller, made the comment:

> Every day, every week, every month, every quarter, the most widely read journals seem just now to vie with each other in telling us that the time for religion is past, that faith is a hallucination or an infantile disease, that the gods have at last been found out and exploded.[17]

That was written almost a century and a half ago, and half a century ago a reviewer wrote of the book, *Ten Growing Soviet Churches* (the very title demonstrates how sudden and unexpected changes can occur), by Michael and Lorna Bordeaux:

> A wide variety of 'churches' has been chosen to represent the vitality of Christianity within the alien environment of a totalitarian state …. From Methodists to Orthodox, facts are presented that illustrate the foolishness of Kruschev's boast that he would exhibit the last Soviet Christian on Soviet TV in 1965![18]

In the words of the reformer, Theodore Beza, 'the church is an anvil that has worn out many hammers'[19]—not because of the superior strength or administrative ability of the human organization, but because of the power of the living God. Jesus said, 'I will build my church, and the gates of hell shall not prevail against it' (Matthew 16:18), and the last book of the Bible, written when the church was under enormous pressure, prophesies (it is expressed in the present tense, so certain is it of fulfilment), 'The kingdom of the world has become the kingdom of our Lord and of his Christ, and he shall reign for ever and ever' (Revelation 11:15).

There really is no need to tremble for the ark of God (1 Samuel 4:13), and yet it remains true that times of doubt may arise. And if such moments creep up on us sometimes, it is instructive to know that some of the people in the Bible were also subject to such moments of questioning. The faith which is so powerfully proclaimed and illustrated in the pages of Scripture is no facile easy belief, much less a cop-out from the realities of life. We can be thankful that the Bible is realistic and honest enough to face up to the doubts of many of its characters; may it bring us all into the category of those of whom Jesus said (in response to the disciple commonly called Doubting Thomas), 'Blessed are those who have not seen and yet have believed' (John 20:29).

## The uses of doubt

This book is written from the point of view of assured faith. In no way does it glory in doubt or suggest that there is something laudable or meritorious about it, as if we all somehow *ought* to have gone through storms of doubt. These chapters do not suggest that there is some virtue *per se* in doubting.

In terms of personal testimony, I am one who was brought up from my earliest days to believe in God. I did not go through any teenage rebellion and I am thankful to have been blessed with faith throughout my life. Because of that background, I was very interested to read a similar testimony in a biography of one of my theological teachers, Professor Tom Torrance. He wrote, 'Through my missionary parents I was imbued from my earliest days with a vivid belief in God. Belief in God was so natural that I could no more doubt the existence of God than the existence of my parents or the world around me. I cannot remember ever having had any doubts about God.'[20]

That did not mean that he understood everything about God or knew all the answers to all the questions that can be asked, but it speaks of an underlying attitude of faith that could withstand the objections and 'shine through the cloud and rain, through sorrow, toil and pain, making the pathway plain'.[21]

Torrance also said, 'Moreover, as long as I can recall, my religious outlook was essentially biblical and evangelical, and indeed evangelistic.' This book is written from such a biblical, evangelical and evangelistic perspective. My hope is that it might lead sceptics to what G. K. Chesterton called the 'first wild doubts of doubt'[22] and then lead on to faith in 'the God and Father of our Lord Jesus Christ' (2 Corinthians 1:3; Ephesians 1:3; 1 Peter 1:3).

It can happen, and Alister McGrath has given an intriguing instance of it. He wrote, 'The ironic fact is that New Atheist anger at the persistence of faith has inadvertently stirred huge interest in the whole God question.' He had given a lecture in London in 2010 and afterwards was approached by a young man who asked him to sign a copy of one of his books. His account goes on: 'He told me that he'd read Richard Dawkins' book, *The God Delusion*, a year or so earlier and it seemed so unfair and one-sided that he felt he needed to hear the other side. So, he started going to church. After a while he found he could not sustain his faith in the parody when confronted with the real thing. He converted to Christianity—joyfully and decisively. "Without Dawkins," he told me, "I would never have given God a second thought".'

McGrath concludes with this tongue-in-cheek reflection: 'As I signed the book the young man told me that he had a theological question for me. Since *The God Delusion* had been instrumental in his conversion, should he thank God for Richard Dawkins in his prayers? I'm still thinking about that one.'[23]

## Assurance

A very different book, and one of the most remarkable ever written, is *The Pilgrim's Progress*. John Bunyan wrote it in 1678—it has been translated into more than 200 languages and it has never been out of print for all of these 345 years. It is an allegory of the Christian life and it tells of a man called Christian who is burdened by his sin. He meets 'Evangelist' who directs him to the cross of Christ, where the burden falls from Christian's back and rolls down the hill into the open grave below.

One edition of the book has an introduction which points out that after Christian's conversion, two-thirds of the book is still to come. 'Christian has received an assurance of grace ... But many of the most desperate adventures with the forces of doubt and despair lie ahead: this is not the end of the drama but the beginning.'[24]

Bunyan included Doubting Castle in his account of the pilgrim way and reflects the fact that many Christians struggle (occasionally or frequently, partly depending on their temperament) with doubts and questions—questions such as:

- Am I one of the chosen?

- How can I know I am saved?
- Will I be able to keep it up?
- What if I let Him down?
- Is it all just a fad (as some of my family and friends suggest)?

There are also the more 'intellectual' issues of how faith relates to scientific studies; how faith can be sustained in the face of suffering and evil; how we deal with injustices perpetrated or condoned by Christians in the past; and so on.

Thankfully we do not have to wait for one-hundred-per-cent clarity on all such personal, social and intellectual questions before we can commit ourselves to Christ. We can come to Him with the attitude of the man who said to Jesus, 'I believe; help my unbelief!' (Mark 9:24). Eugene Peterson's *The Message* paraphrases it as 'I believe. Help me with my doubts!'[25]

In this book we will be considering doubts about particular matters, such as the authority of God's Word, the goodness of God and the reality of Christ's resurrection. But there is also the most fundamental doubt of all: How can I be sure that I am a genuine believer? Is there such a thing as certainty about salvation? Can I know that I will go to heaven and be with Christ? Does the sentiment of Fanny Crosby's famous hymn 'Blessed Assurance' amount to arrogance and presumption?[26]

In 1 John 5:13, we read, 'I write these things to you who believe in the name of the Son of God, that you may know that you have eternal life.' John's Gospel was written to bring its readers to faith in the first place—'that you may believe that Jesus is the Christ, the Son of God, and that by believing you may have life in his name' (John 20:31). Then, this epistle was written so that believers may have assurance. The Greek for 'to know' is found no less than twenty-five times in the five chapters.

The whole message of the gospel is about a salvation that is entirely the gift of God—something to be received, not achieved: 'For by grace you have been saved through faith. And this is not your own doing; it is the gift of God, not a result of works, so that no one may boast' (Ephesians 2:8–9). There is nothing presumptuous or arrogant about the claim to have an assurance of salvation and an assurance about heaven.

Some people have even found that they have emerged from periods of questioning and doubt with a stronger faith than before. I was interested to read of a theologian who had spoken at an American university and who was approached by one of the students afterwards. The student said, 'I have often desired such an opportunity as this but have always been afraid to express my doubts to those who could best relieve them, lest I should ... forfeit the esteem of those whom I revere.' The theologian responded by saying, 'Ministers of the gospel have wrestled with too many doubts, in reaching their conclusions, not to sympathize with the early struggles of others in the search after truth.' He then added, 'Doubt is but the hunger of the mind, the starting point of all enquiry.'[27]

It is possible to be a Christian and yet to lack assurance, but we know from His Word (and from 1 John in particular) that God's desire is that His people should have an underlying assurance. '... Those who truly believe in the Lord Jesus, and love him in sincerity, endeavouring to walk in all good conscience before him, may in this life be certainly assured that they are in the state of grace, and may rejoice in the hope of the glory of God.'[28]

This assurance is both *objective* and *subjective*.

Objectively, it is based on the Word and promises of God. He wants us to rely on *His* promises rather than *our* feelings. There is a nineteenth-century hymn on this subject which is worded in ways that may sound rather quaint to us now, but they are well worth pondering:

> 'Twixt gleams of joy and clouds of doubt
> Our feelings come and go;
> Our best estate is tossed about
> In ceaseless ebb and flow.
> No mood of feeling, form of thought,
> Is constant for a day;
> But Thou, O Lord, Thou changest not:
> The same Thou art alway.
>
> … Let me no more my comfort draw
> From my frail hold of Thee,
> In this alone rejoice with awe –
> Thy mighty grasp of me.

The last verse takes account of the fact that times of uncertainty may sometimes afflict Christians, but it says:

> Thy purpose of eternal good
> Let me but surely know;
> On this I'll lean—let changing mood
> And feeling come and go –
> Glad when Thy sunshine fills my soul,
> Not lorn when clouds o'ercast,
> Since Thou within Thy sure control
> Of love dost hold me fast.[29]

Another hymn, which has become popular in recent times, says:

> Those He saves are His delight;
> Christ will hold me fast.
> He'll not let my soul be lost;
> His promises shall last.
> He will hold me fast.[30]

Picture a little child crossing a busy street with her father, and imagine someone saying to her, 'Aren't you afraid that you might let go of your father's hand amid all these cars?' I imagine her replying, 'But I'm not holding on to my father; my father is holding on to me.' The application is clear—He will hold us fast.

Assurance is based, firstly, on the Word and promises of God, which are 'trustworthy and true' (Revelation 22:6). Here is a selection of such promises that give assurance to believers:

- 'My sheep hear my voice, and I know them, and they follow me. I give them eternal life, and they will never perish, and no one will snatch them out of my hand' (John 10:27–28).
- 'Whoever hears my word and believes him who sent me has eternal life. He does not come into judgement, but has passed from death to life' (John 5:24).
- 'If we confess our sins, he is faithful and just to forgive us our sins and to cleanse us from all unrighteousness' (1 John 1:9).
- 'I am with you always, to the end of the age' (Matthew 28:20).
- 'God so loved the world, that he gave his only Son, that whoever believes in him should not perish but have eternal life' (John 3:16).
- 'If you confess with your mouth that Jesus is Lord and believe

in your heart that God raised him from the dead, you will be saved' (Romans 10:9).

- 'He who began a good work in you will bring it to completion at the day of Jesus Christ' (Philippians 1:6).

Why should we doubt these royal promises? Such words give objective grounds for true assurance.

This is sometimes represented in the simple illustration of three people walking in single file along a narrow ridge. At the front is *Fact*, in the middle is *Faith* and in the rear is *Feeling*. The Christian is represented by Faith, and if Faith keeps turning to check that Feeling is coming along, that increases the possibility of losing balance and stumbling. The best thing for Faith to do is to keep his eyes on Fact in front and leave Feeling to come along behind.

'Lack of assurance', Sinclair Ferguson has written, 'is often caused, like a sense of inferiority, by being too taken up with ourselves. But our assurance does not lie in what we are, be we great or small. It lies in what God has done in his plan of salvation to secure us to himself. "Believe God's Word and power more than you believe your own feelings and experiences," wrote Samuel Rutherford to a correspondent.'[31]

Having said that, it is true there is also a subjective element in assurance, and 1 John is the go-to book to learn about it. John gives various signs by which we may know that we are truly saved and assured of eternal life. It is not a matter of receiving salvation by grace and then assurance by our works. To read Scripture that way would be a complete misunderstanding. It is rather that there are certain signs which confirm to us that we are truly on the Christian path. They are not the *grounds* of salvation but the *evidence* of it. As these evidences are real in our lives, we may come to an assured faith that we truly are Christians and give thanks and glory to God for His great salvation.

It should be noted also that these evidences are for us to apply to ourselves, not other people. They are not given so that we can sit in judgement on other people. It is not for us to judge anyone ('The Lord knows those who are his'—2 Timothy 2:19) but 1 John gives us three lines of evidence by which we may be assured of our salvation. They are theological, ethical and social—or, more simply, they relate to our belief in God's truth, our obedience to God's commands and our love for God's people.[32]

a) Belief in God's truth. Several times in 1 John we find this emphasis. It is most plainly stated in 5:1: 'Everyone who believes that Jesus is the Christ has been born of God.' 4:1–2 says, 'Beloved, do not believe every spirit, but test the spirits to see whether they are from God, for many false prophets have gone out into the world. By this you know the Spirit of God: every spirit that confesses that Jesus Christ has come in the flesh is from God.'

John Newton wrote the pertinent lines:

> What think ye of Christ? is the test
> To try both your state and your scheme;
> You cannot be right in the rest
> Unless you think rightly of him.[33]

Belief in Jesus as merely a fine teacher and good example, is not Christian belief; the gospel is about the incarnation of Jesus, with all that this means in terms of the unique combination in Him of real humanity and divine nature; because He is divine, He can *save* us, and because He is human, He can save *us*.

Belief in God's truth is one indication of real Christianity. Under the Spirit's inspiration, John writes, 'Whoever knows God listens to us; whoever is not from God does not listen to us. By this we know the Spirit of truth and the spirit of error' (1 John 4:6). Jesus said that He would lead His apostles in recording His teaching (John 14:26, 16:13) and a mark of real spiritual life is a desire to know and trust that teaching.

b) Obedience to God's commands. We may test ourselves by whether our earnest desire is to bring every part of our lives into captivity to Christ in obedience (2 Corinthians 10:5): 'We know that we have come to know him', John writes, 'if we keep his commandments. Whoever says, "I know him" but does not keep his commandments is a liar... By this we may know that we are in him: whoever says he abides in him ought to walk in the same way in which he walked' (1 John 2:3–6). We cannot 'say we have fellowship with him while we walk in darkness' (1 John 1:6).

John says, 'No one who abides in him keeps on sinning' (3:6). None of us is perfect, and there will be lapses and times when Christians have to come to God in repentance. The beginning of chapter 2 says, 'I am writing these things to you so that you may not sin. But if anyone does sin, we have an advocate with the Father, Jesus Christ the righteous' (2:1). This will be true so long as we are in this life, but the basic desire to please God and live in His way is another indication of real Christianity.

c) Love for God's people. Here is another evidence of salvation. 'We know that we have passed out of death into life, because we love the brothers' (3:14). Delight in Christian fellowship is an indication of real spiritual life, and real believers will adhere to the church (even with all its faults). If people reject the family of God, it shows that they were not really part of it in the first place: 'They went out from us, but they were not of us; for if they had been of us, they would have continued with us' (2:19).

These are three lines of evidence by which we can have assurance of being truly saved. As we believe in God's truth, live by God's commands and love God's people, we are assured that we really do belong to Christ. These are means by which the Spirit gives the inner conviction of belonging to Christ. These things work out John's whole purpose in writing: 'that you may know that you have eternal life' (5:13).

The rest of this book is about threats to that assurance—times of doubt—and it is to be hoped that the consideration of some biblical examples of people whose faith was tried and tested will help to initiate and sustain true and assured faith in the living God.

**NOTES**

1 From a song in *Porgy And Bess* by George and Ira Gershwin

2 *Mere Christianity* (London: Collins, 1966; originally published in 1952), p. 121.

3 I am using the word 'apologist' to refer to someone who seeks to defend the reasonableness of faith (see 1 Peter 3:15).

4 Lewis, C. S., *Mere Christianity*, p. 121.

5 D'Souza, Dinesh, *What's So Great About Christianity?* (Washington, DC: Regnery Publishing, 2007), p. 36, (commenting on the views of Daniel Dennett and Richard Rorty).

6 Quoted from the Authorised King James Version; the Greek for 'darkly' is *en ainigmati*, from which we get the English 'enigmatic'. The ESV translates verse 9–10, 'For we know in part and we prophesy in part, but when the perfect comes, the partial will pass away.'

7   Hymn, 'The Sands of Time', by Anne Ross Cousin, 1824–1906.

8   John Murray, *The Attestation of Scripture in The Infallible Word*, (Westminster Theological Seminary, 1946), pp. 7–8 (Murray was writing about the doctrine of Scripture in particular but the principle can be applied to issues of faith generally). Similarly, Sinclair Ferguson has commented on John Owen's confession that he was not sure of the meaning of a particular text: 'If Owen had the wisdom and courage to say, "I am not completely certain what this text of Scripture means," we should not be slow to share his modesty, Indeed, it is one of the blessings of Reformed theology's sense of the incomprehensible greatness of God that it recognizes we do not know all of the answers!' Sinclair B. Ferguson, *Some Pastors And Teachers*, (Edinburgh: Banner of Truth, 2017), p. 258.

9   Alex McLellan took the title of his book from this incident: *A Jigsaw Guide to Making Sense of the World*, (Downers Grove, Illinois: IVP, 2012), pp. 11–12.

10  Hymn by Benjamin Mansell Ramsey, 1849–1923.

11  Quoted in: H. W. Griffin, *The Authentic Voice*, (Tring, Herts: Lion, 1988), pp. 85–6. In a similar vein, the famous novelist, Robert Louis Stevenson, who rejected the faith in which he had been reared, once wrote in a letter, 'It was really pathetic to hear my father praying pointedly for me today at family worship, and to think the poor man's supplications were addressed to nothing better able to hear and answer than the chandelier.' (Quoted by Iain H. Murray in *The Undercover Revolution*, (Edinburgh: Banner of Truth, 2009), p. 13.

12  Unsourced quotation given in frontispiece of: Os Guinness, *Doubt*, (Berkhamsted, Lion Publishing, 1976).

13  Stott, John, *Through the Bible Through the Year* (Oxford: Lion Hudson, 2006), p. 319.

14  For example, I noticed a footnote in Richard Dawkins' book, *The God Delusion*, (London: Bantam Press, 2006), in which he referred to the growth of certain cults in Vanuatu (formerly the New Hebrides) where missionaries had been at work (such as John G. Paton of *Thirty Years Among South Sea Cannibals* fame) and he could not resist remarking that the islands had long been 'infested' with missionaries (p. 236). The same man has referred to teaching children the Bible as abusive, provoking the refreshingly outspoken Melanie Phillips to write an article (published on 23rd December 2012 in the *Daily Mail*) headed, 'Oh, do put a sock in it, you atheist Scrooge!'

15  Randall, David J., *Why we (still) believe*, (Fearn, Ross-shire: Christian Focus, 2017).

16  *Evangelicals Now*, March 2018, p.28.

17  Article in *Princeton Theological Seminary Bulletin* XI,1, 1990.

18  Review in *Arena* of: Bordeaux, Michael and Lorna, *Ten Growing Soviet Churches*, published by MARC Europe, 1987.

19  https://www.oxfordreference.com/display/10.1093/acref/9780198734901.001.0001/acref-9780198734901-e-365 (accessed 12.9.23)

20 Quoted in: McGrath, A., *T. F. Torrance—An Intellectual Biography* (Edinburgh: T & T Clark, 1999), p. 13.

21 (Adapted) lines from the hymn, 'Teach my Thy Way', already cited.

22 Chesterton, C. K., *Orthodoxy*, (Mineola, New York: Dover Publications edition, 2004), p. 77.

23 McGrath, Alister, *Why God Won't Go Away*, (London: SPCK, 2011), pp. 98–99.

24 Sharrock, Roger, *Introduction to The Pilgrim's Progress* by John Bunyan, (Harmondsworth: Penguin Books edition, 1965), p. 19.

25 Petersen, Eugene, *The Message*, (Colorado Springs: Navpress, 1993), p. 110.

26 That very hymn actually precludes any such charge. Its first verse refers to the Christian as an 'heir of salvation' (an heir inherits something from someone else), the 'purchase of God' (salvation is His doing), 'born of His Spirit' (people cannot give birth to themselves) and 'washed in His blood' (also about what God has done).

27 Palmer, Benjamin Morgan, *Selected Writings* (Edinburgh: Banner of Truth, 2014), p. 18.

28 Westminster Confession of Faith, XVIII, p. 1.

29 Hymn by John Campbell Shairp, 1819–85.

30 Hymn by Ada R. Habershon, 1861–1918.

31 Ferguson, Sinclair B., *The Christian Life*, (Edinburgh: Banner of Truth, 2013 edition), p. 24f.

32 David Watson summarized these evidences in a different way: 'John gives us at least eight signs of a healthy spiritual life: a new family (1:7), a new obedience (2:3), a new love for God (2:15–17), a new hatred for sin (3:9), a new love for other Christians (3:14), a new peace (3:21), a new enemy (3:8), and a new power over evil (5:4).' That summary would make a good basis for a Bible study. Watson, David, *Live A New Life*, (Leicester: IVP, 1975), pp. 24–28.

33 Hymn by John Newton, 1725–1807, 'What Think Ye Of Christ?' https://hymnary.org/text/what_think_ye_of_christ_is_the_test (accessed 7.9.23)

# 1 'Did God really say...?'

## DOUBTS ABOUT THE AUTHORITY OF GOD'S WORD

'If this book works as I intend', wrote one of today's most famous atheists, 'religious readers who open it will be atheists when they put it down.'[1] Has his hope been realized? I have not heard of any such result, and the story told in the introductory chapter shows that it can work in reverse! Such intemperate lambasting of Christianity can actually evoke more sympathetic assessments than conversions to atheism. If something is worthy of such vitriol as he has dished out, it must be worth attacking!

When it comes to the Bible, obviously it is God's intention that atheists and unbelievers who open it will become believers as they read its story. In the introduction, I quoted the apostle John's statement of his purpose. In the last verse of his Gospel, he referred to the fact that Jesus did many things that have not been reported—which stands to reason really; there must have been hundreds of things Jesus said and did that have not been recorded.

So how did John select his material? He tells us it was 'that you may believe that Jesus is the Christ, the Son of God, and that by believing you may have life in his name' (John 20:31). Such was his goal and by a legitimate extension that could be said to be the goal of the whole Bible.

There are many kinds of writing in the Bible. Its message is conveyed through historical writing (like Samuel, Kings and

Chronicles), through poetry (like Psalms and Proverbs), through apocalyptic visions (like Revelation), and the individual books need to be read for what they are, not for what they are not. You do not read the telephone book in the same way as you read a detective novel, or an academic treatise like you read the weather forecast; similarly, you cannot read *Job* in the same way as you read *Matthew*, or *Ecclesiastes* in the same way as *Ephesians*. If you were to read the book, *The Hound of the Baskervilles* to learn about dogs, or *Heart of Midlothian* to learn about an Edinburgh football team, you would be very disappointed!

The Bible is a book about God. It is inspired by God to make us 'wise for salvation through faith in Christ Jesus' (2 Timothy 3:15), and yet, it is striking that it does not begin by setting out on page one a set of arguments for the existence of God. It simply says, 'In the beginning God created the heavens and the earth' (Genesis 1:1) and it proceeds with the narrative of the ways in which God has revealed Himself.

It takes for granted the fact that we could have no knowledge of God if God had not made Himself known, and it asserts that He has made Himself known:

- in the works of creation (Psalm 19:1)
- in the sense of the eternal that he has implanted in us (Ecclesiastes 3:11)
- in the pages of Scripture (2 Timothy 3:16)
- and, of course, in the person and work of Jesus Christ (Hebrews 1:2).

However, alongside the encouragements to believe, we see a number of instances of doubt and, very near the beginning

(Genesis 3:1), we hear the voice of the tempter questioning God's instructions—'Did God actually say ...?' In verse 4 of that chapter we find him contradicting God's Word—'You will not surely die,' and then suggesting that if you rebel against God 'you will be like God' (v. 5).

It is a sequence: doubt—denial—defiance. Doubt about God's Word leads to the denial of His truth, and denial of His truth leads to outright defiance of His will. The devil used doubt to lead Adam and Eve into unbelief and rebellion.

Most people would probably presume that doubt is the opposite of faith. That, on the one hand, there are people who are supposedly undisturbed by any questions—people who would be dismissed by opponents as blinkered believers—and, on the other hand, there are the people who are bothered by all sorts of questions and problems about believing.

But in reality, the opposite of faith is not doubt; the opposite of faith is unbelief. Os Guinness' book on the subject has the sub-title, *Faith in two minds*. Doubt lies in between faith and unbelief and, when it comes, there are two possibilities. It can lead to unbelief and rejection of faith in God, or the doubter can come through it with a stronger faith—it might be likened to coming out of a cloud of fog into clear sunshine.

In the introduction, I referred to C. S. Lewis' reflection on his pre-Christian past when he wrote, 'Now that I am a Christian, I do have moods in which the whole thing looks very improbable but when I was an atheist I had moods in which Christianity looked terribly probable!'[2] Many people pass through times when their

Christianity looks rather improbable; something happens and an element of doubt is raised so that they wonder about it all.

The second half of Lewis' statement gives us a prayer topic for unbelievers we know—that they would come to experience doubts about their atheism and unbelief[3]; that they would experience what the poet, Robert Browning, called the 'Grand Perhaps':

> How can we guard our unbelief,
> Make it bear fruit to us?– the problem here.
> Just when we are safest, there's a sunset-touch,
> A fancy from a flower-bell, some one's death,
> A chorus-ending from Euripides,–
> And that's enough for fifty hopes and fears
> As old and new at once as Nature's self,
> To rap and knock and enter in our soul.[4]

Are doubts to lead to unbelief or belief—to the rejection of faith or a strengthened faith?

Adam and Eve were placed in a wonderful garden with freedom to enjoy the things that God had made, except for one thing: 'You may surely eat of every tree of the garden, but of the tree of the knowledge of good and evil you shall not eat, for in the day that you eat of it you shall surely die' (Genesis 2:16–17). We later discover that the reference is to that spiritual death which would mean alienation from God—the estrangement that we see when 'the man and his wife hid themselves from the presence of the Lord God among the trees of the garden'[5] (Genesis 3:8).

And when we look at the beginning of Genesis 3, it is instructive to see the way in which doubt would be used by the devil to entice them towards unbelief—which is no ancient story. Of course, it *is* an ancient story. The New Testament clearly regards Adam and Eve as historical characters (not mythical representations)[6] and here they are confronted with the temptation, and they yield to it and fall from grace. This was the introduction of sin and death into the world. The devil used doubt to lead them to deny the Word of the Lord, ignore the warning of the Lord and reject the way of the Lord.

### Denial of God's Word

'Did God actually say ...?' is the word of the tempter in Genesis 3:1.[7] We are told that the serpent was more crafty than any other beast God had made, and he did not come straight at Eve with a message that said, 'Listen, Eve, all that God has said is a load of rubbish.'

There is a subtlety about it and, of course, as Eve points out, it's a misquotation. It is commonly said that the devil can quote (or misquote) Scripture for his own ends[8] and here he misrepresents God's Word as, 'You shall not eat of any tree in the garden.' In truth, God had not said that they were not to eat from *any* tree; it was rather an instruction not to eat of a particular tree.

Then follows the outright denial of God's message. 'The serpent said to the woman, "You will not surely die. For God knows that when you eat of it your eyes will be opened, and *you* will be like God' (Genesis 3:4–5; italic emphasis mine).

The temptation that faced Adam and Eve in the garden is the temptation that faces people in all generations—to think that we can sit in judgement on God's Word and suppose that we know better than He does. Sometimes it comes along the lines, 'Times have changed, and how can you believe that a book written all these centuries ago could possibly be a message for this twenty-first century?'

One of the strongest evidences for its veracity and authority is the simple fact that it survives; more than that, it lives and breathes still and still changes lives, bringing people to faith, nurturing faith in believers and bringing a message of light, peace and comfort.

It has its own internal power, as Charles Spurgeon emphasized when he was asked how he would defend the Bible. He responded, 'Defend it? I would as soon defend a roaring lion.' It suggests a ridiculous picture, as if someone would address a lion and say, 'O little lion, don't worry; I'm here to defend you.' He said, 'Let it out; it will defend itself.'

Yet still there is the voice that whispers, 'Did God actually say … You will not surely die.' That voice comes to people in different ways—sometimes through intellectual doubts raised by this or that branch of study; sometimes through a plain unwillingness to believe it is God's Word because of the implications for our lives and behaviour; sometimes through explanations more or less psychological, that purport to tell us what is *really* going on.

When I started as a student at Edinburgh University, one of the first debates I saw advertised was on the motion, 'That Christianity is intellectual suicide?' Well of course it is not; we are not called to suspend all rational powers and ignore all challenges. We are to love the Lord God with all our mind as well as all our heart, soul and strength (Mark 12:30), and when we say that it was the devil who introduced this doubt, we are not saying that we ought to refuse to think about our faith and the authoritative claims of the Bible.

F. F. Bruce was a Biblical scholar in Manchester who spoke of being asked sometimes whether he felt a tension between his academic study of the Bible in a university context and his own personal approach to the Bible as a devout Christian. His answer was:

> I should not find the career of a Bible teacher so satisfying as I do if I were not persuaded that the Bible is God's Word written. The fact that I am so persuaded means that I must not come to the Bible with my own preconceptions of what the Bible, as God's Word written, can or cannot say. It is important to determine, by the canons of grammatical, textual, historical and literary study, what it actually does say.[9]

Such is the reflection of a man who was a leading scholar of the Bible and also a committed Christian. Few could match his scholarliness, and the point is that such study of the Bible is not prohibited by saying that it is the devil who introduces this doubt in his, 'Did God actually say …?', and who uses such methods to lead to the denial of God's Word.

When we know *what* the Bible says and recognize that it *is* God's Word, we are not to listen to the voice that says, 'Yes, but …'. Clearly it is not wrong to be tempted; it is what we do in response to temptation that is important.

## Ignoring God's warning

The serpent moved from the subtle doubt ('Did God say …?') to outright contradiction ('You will not die'). For Eve there was a choice: on one side, there was the voice of God saying, 'Of the tree of the knowledge of good and evil you shall not eat, for in the day that you eat of it you shall surely die', and on the other side was the voice of the devil saying, 'You will not surely die.'

Which was she to believe? Verse 6 tells us, 'When the woman saw that the tree was good for food, and that it was a delight to the eyes, and that the tree was to be desired to make one wise, she took of its fruit and ate, and she also gave some to her husband who was with her, and he ate.'

The following verse tells of the immediate disruption that was brought in by that disobedience. Many people who have only a casual knowledge of Scripture suppose that the temptation of the garden of Eden had something to do with sex ('forbidden fruit' and all that). It did not. The temptation was the temptation to defy God and His Word. But perhaps that mistaken view has been based on what the next verse says about their eyes being opened, 'and they knew that they were naked'—which they did not seem to have noticed previously! Prior to this point, 'naked' was a word without any meaning; there was no such concept. But the Fall (as we call it) had ended innocence and brought in the whole concept of shame. Sin spoils everything.

That is the teaching and the warning of Scripture. God's warnings are for our good, and defying His warnings spoils things.

It seems pretty obvious that the world is spoiled by sin; I have heard an atheist speak about how we're all pretty decent people, but such optimism seems rather trite and misplaced when we consider the whole story of man's inhumanity to man. People may deny the concept of sin, re-define it, or imply that if we could just forget about God and the shackles of morality, then we could re-create paradise, but all such notions founder on the simple facts of the matter. This is a spoiled world; it is a world of violence and crime, a world that *ought* to be a place of peace, harmony and delight—yet the life of man (as Thomas Hobbes expressed it) is 'solitary, poor, nasty, brutish and short'.[10]

Adam and Eve disobeyed and their disobedience has cast a long shadow over all generations since. We are all infected with the genetic tendency to rebel, to ignore God's warnings, to think that we know best. Jesus said about judging others' sins, 'Let him who is without sin among you be the first to throw a stone' (John 8:7), making the point that we are all sinners; we have all succumbed to the devil's temptations. We know the voice that says, 'Oh come on, Eve; you don't want to believe all that stuff; it's all just words to scare you into obedience but nothing will happen if you just eat the forbidden fruit.'

## Rejection of God's way

The denial of God's Word and the ignoring of His warnings, result in the rejection of the way of the Lord. That rejection is typified in the now famous song, 'My Way', which expresses the sentiment of someone facing the end of this life. But what could be more tragic when we come to the end of our lives than to simply say that we did things in our own way?

Against such an attitude stands the Bible's word: 'There is a way that seems right to a man, but its end is the way to death' (Proverbs 14:12). That is the story of Eden and it is the abiding truth about all rejection of God's way in favour of 'my way'.

I once attempted a Christianized version of the song along the following lines. I do not expect it to feature in the charts!—but I suggest it as a better attitude with which to face life and death. It could be entitled, 'Your Way':

And now, dear Lord in heaven,
We come to pray and seek your blessing;
To You we turn, almighty God,
The Lord of love, the great Creator.
Help us to live a life that's full,
A life that finds its point and purpose
Not in ourselves but, Lord,
In finding *Your way*.

And when our lives shall end,
And when we face the final curtain,
Give us, dear Lord, the hope we need,
To trust in Your forgiving mercy,
That by Your grace we look ahead,
To endless days in endless glory,
And all through Christ our Lord;
We trust in *Your way*.

We have already quoted the hymn that says, 'When doubts and fear arise, teach me Thy way.' That is the Christian answer to the temptation of Genesis 3:5: 'When you eat of it your eyes will be opened, and you will be like God.'

Later, after the Genesis flood had ushered in a new beginning, we read of the tower of Babel when people said to one another, 'Come, let us build ourselves a city and a tower with its top in the heavens, and let us make a name for ourselves' (Genesis 11:4). Obviously, there is nothing wicked about town planning or civil engineering; the problem was in the motivation. They were concerned to assert themselves, and that story continues through the pages of Scripture.

It finds expression in the rich farmer of Jesus' parable. He was rich and successful, and there was nothing wrong with that; his tragic and sinful error was to be full of self. 'He thought to himself, "What shall I do, for I have nowhere to store my crops?" And he said, "I will do this: I will tear down my barns and build larger ones, and there I will store all my grain and my goods. And I will say to my soul, 'Soul, you have ample goods laid up for many years; relax, eat, drink, be merry'"' (Luke 12:17–21).

It is full of 'I', 'my' and 'myself', and the tragedy was that he missed out the most important things of all. He ignored God; he forgot that it is appointed for all of us to die and then give account of our lives (Hebrews 9:27; Revelation 20:12–15); he was destroyed by the cancerous disease of sin.

Genesis does not tell of the enemy suggesting that there is no such being as God; he simply appeals to human pride—the desire to assert ourselves—allied perhaps with the idea that God is really just a spoilsport who wants to cramp our style. When he says, 'God knows that when you eat of it your eyes will be opened, and you will be like God' (verse 5)—of course God knows no such thing. It is the opposite of the truth. If we rebel against God, then far from being *like* God, we will be estranged *from* God. It is the rebel against God who is blind, as John Newton (1725–1807) so famously expressed it:

> Amazing grace, how sweet the sound
> That saved a wretch like me;
> I once was lost but now am found,
> Was blind, but now I see.

Looking back, he realized that it was when he asserted his own independence and rebelled against God that he was blind.

Firstly, there was the attack on God and His Word; then there was the assault on faith in that Word; and now there is the appeal to our human pride.

Much more could be said (and has been said!) about Genesis 3—the fall and the setting of the scene for everything else in the Bible: God's great plan of rescue and salvation. We sometimes sing about it: 'O wisest love that flesh and blood which did in Adam fail'—that is Genesis 3; 'Should strive afresh against the foe, should strive and should prevail'[11]—that is the gospel.

That second Adam faced temptation too—temptation as a human being to doubt the Father's Word and go a different way. Right at the beginning of His public ministry, which was to culminate in the cross where He died in our place, the devil sought to turn Him aside from the path He had come to tread.

It is an interesting parallel. We have considered the beginnings of everything in the garden where the devil succeeded in using doubt to lead people astray; now, at the beginning of Jesus' ministry, we see a similar attempt to turn things a different way. But the devil failed. The flesh and blood which failed in Adam, now resisted the temptation and prevailed against the foe.

Matthew 4:3-9 tells of the tempter using the same little word as he used in Eden—the word, 'if':

- '*If* you are the Son of God, command these stones to become loaves of bread.'
- '*If* you are the Son of God, throw yourself down' (and test God's word about protecting you).
- 'All the kingdoms of the world and their glory I will give you, *if* you will fall down and worship me.'

So, Jesus was tempted—to deny the Word of the Lord and reject the way of the Lord. And, of course, each time Jesus answered by standing firm on God's Word.

The devil's word is, 'Has God said ...?' Jesus' answer is, 'God has said ...!' Three times over we see it (vv. 4, 7, 10):

- 'It is written, "Man shall not live by bread alone, but by every word that comes from the mouth of God."'
- 'It is written, "You shall not put the Lord your God to the test."'
- 'It is written, "You shall worship the Lord your God and him only shall you serve."'

There is the Son of God, armed with the Word of God, refusing to be turned aside from the way of God. Right through to the end of His struggle, He met it—the voice that came to Him even on the cross: 'If you are the Son of God, come down from the cross' (Matthew 27:40).

Instead of denying the Word of the Lord, we are encouraged to stand on it; instead of ignoring the warnings of the Lord, we are to pay heed to what He tells us; instead of rejecting the way of the Lord, we should seek His help to follow Him always.

The subject of this first chapter is fundamentally important since confidence in the truth and reliability of the Bible underpins everything else in Christianity and conversely, doubts about the Bible will undermine faith. The Bible is God's Word—'men spoke from God as they were carried along by the Holy Spirit' (2 Peter 1:21)—and its authority is confirmed:

- by the testimony of the ages,
- by the testimony of the Bible itself,

- by the testimony of Jesus and
- by the inner testimony of the Holy Spirit.

I have written elsewhere about this subject:

> It is not a matter of taking the Bible 'literally'—we know what Jesus meant, for example, when he said, 'I am the vine' (John 15:5). Nor does a 'high' view of Scripture mean that everything written in the Bible is for emulation; many things are recorded without any implication that they should be repeated or copied (or example, in John 2:15 we are told that Jesus made a whip, but we are not told to go and do likewise). Not all parts of Scripture are equally easy to understand and, the fact that every part of Scripture is equally inspired, does not mean that all are equally 'inspiring' (genealogical lists, for example—although they also have their importance). There are parts of Scripture that we find difficult, but one is often reminded of the remark attributed to Mark Twain that the parts of the Bible which bothered him were not the parts he did not understand but the parts he did understand only too well![12]

However, this book does not go into detail on such questions and, since it is such an important subject, it may be helpful to suggest some further reading on these themes:

- John Blanchard, *Why Believe The Bible?* (Darlington: Evangelical Press, 2004).
- Amy Orr-Ewing, *Why Trust the Bible?* (Leicester: IVP, 2005).
- Sinclair B. Ferguson, *From the Mouth of God* (Edinburgh: Banner of Truth, 2014).

**NOTES**

1  Dawkins, Richard, *The God Delusion*, (London: Black Swan, 2007), p. 28, (first published by

Bantam Press in 2006).

2 Lewis, C. S., *Mere Christianity*, (London: Fontana edition 1966; originally published 1952), p. 121.

3 Like the intelligent young man who attended a *Christianity Explored* group and commented afterwards, 'I'm an atheist, but I'm beginning to have my doubts.'—Robertson, David, *The Dawkins Letters*, (Fearn: Christian Focus, 2007), p. 16.

4 *Bishop Blougram's Apology* by Robert Browning (1812–1889).

5 Is this a Bible joke (as if anyone can hide from God)?

6 For Example, Romans 5:12–21.

7 Carl Trueman has described these words as 'the first apparent deconstructive reading of a text'—that is, the separation of the intention of the speaker from the response in the mind of the hearer or reader. 'It is clear that the denial of any role to authorial intent in determining the meaning of a text is lethal to evangelical Christianity. If the meaning of a text is determined by what the individual reader or the reading community "reads into" the said texts, then we are left with a God who simply cannot be known.' *The Wages of Spin*, (Fearn, Ross-shire: Christian Focus, 2004), pp. 55–57.

8 'The devil can cite Scripture for his purpose'—Antonio in Shakespeare's *The Merchant of Venice*, 1, iii, 93.

9 Bruce, F. F., *In Retrospect*, (Glasgow: Pickering & Inglis, 1980), p. 311.

10 Hobbes, Thomas, *Leviathan*, (Everyman edition; originally published 1651), p. 65.

11 Hymn, 'Praise to the Holiest in the height' by John Henry Newman, (1801–90).

12 Randall, David, *A Sad Departure*, (Edinburgh: Banner of Truth, 2015), pp. 90–91.

Please see appendix to chapter 1 on p. 251.

# 2 A human invention?

## DOUBTS ABOUT THE REALITY OF GOD

O ne of the books on my shelves[1] is subtitled, *How the world's most notorious atheist changed his mind.* It is by the late Antony Flew, and the cover of the book has these words in red, 'There Is No God', with the 'No' scored out and 'A' inserted in its place. For much of his life, Flew had been an atheist but he was committed to going where the evidence leads and towards the end of his life said that he was convinced of the existence of God.

He did not actually become a Christian, but that change from 'There Is No God' to 'There Is A God' is very interesting, and it introduces the theme of the reality of God. Is He in fact real, or is the concept of 'God' simply something that human beings have invented?

Interestingly, the early Christians were sometimes accused of being atheists. Amid Roman persecution of Christians in AD 156, the 86-year-old bishop of Smyrna, Polycarp, was brought before a Roman proconsul who tried to persuade Polycarp, especially in view of his age, to comply with what was demanded—to 'swear by the genius of Caesar, repent, say: "Away with the Atheists".'

Polycarp refused to do so, and the ancient record says:

> Polycarp, with a stern countenance looked on all the crowd of lawless heathen in the arena, and waving his hand at them, he groaned and looked up to heaven and said, 'Away with the Atheists'. But when the Proconsul pressed him and said, 'Take the oath and I will let you go,

revile Christ,' Polycarp said, 'For eighty and six years have I been His servant, and He has done me no wrong; how can I blaspheme my King who saved me?[2]

'Atheists'? The enemies of the gospel wanted Polycarp to round on Christians who did not believe in the many gods of Rome and ally himself instead with those who accepted the whole pantheon of gods, supposedly honoured by Rome; we can say 'supposedly' because with many people there was probably little if any personal commitment involved. It meant simply a willingness to toe the line, whereas these stupid Christians actually denied the existence of such gods!

Polycarp, however, turned it round. When he pointed to the crowds and said, 'Away with the atheists', it was a courageous response and also the prelude to his being burned alive, after which we are told that the multitude marvelled at the difference between the unbelievers and the Christians.

How remarkable that a Christian should be accused of being an atheist. (They were also accused of incest, because they talked about loving their brothers and sisters, and of cannibalism, because Jesus said of the bread of communion, 'This is my body; eat of it'!) Perhaps part of the reason for this was the simple fact that nobody could see the God whom the Christians worshipped and served—and they might have said, as many of our contemporaries say, 'If you can't see Him, how do you know He exists?'

Perhaps it was what the people of Israel felt in Exodus 32 when they asked Aaron to make them a god they could see. Their attitude could be paraphrased as: *Where is this God who's supposed to be our*

*God; this God who is supposed to have led Abraham, Isaac and Jacob; this God Moses is always on about? We haven't seen Him, so how do we know He's real?*

They were gathered at the foot of Mount Sinai. Moses seemed to have been on the mountain for a long time and, as they waited, doubts began to creep into the hearts and minds of the people; in fact, they did not just creep in—they swept in like a torrent—and before long the people had allowed these doubts to lead them into unbelief, rebellion and sin. They pressurized Aaron to make for them a god they could *see*.

We have already suggested that doubt is not the opposite of faith, as many assume without too much thought. Just as we say about temptation, that being tempted is not wrong—it all depends on what you do with the temptation—so with doubt. Everything depends on what we do with it.

In the case of Aaron and the Israelites, they sadly allowed doubt to lead them into rebellion and wrongdoing. Exodus 32:1 tells of the people approaching Aaron and saying, 'Up, make us gods who shall go before us. As for this Moses, the man who brought us up out of the land of Egypt, we do not know what has become of him.'

They could not deny that Moses had been a great leader and deliverer, and they may have said, 'It seemed as if God was enabling him to do what he did, but now we don't know what has happened to him and maybe, after all, it was simply through capable human leadership that he achieved what he achieved—maybe there was no need to bring *God* into it.'

They may have sympathized with the nineteenth-century mathematician, Pierre Laplace, who was asked by Napoleon where

God fitted in to his system and famously replied, 'Sir, I have no need of that hypothesis.'[3]

The people, gathered before Aaron, were possibly expressing several 'maybes': *'Maybe we don't need this idea of God being behind everything; maybe Moses has been using the idea of a divine Being to keep us in line; maybe Moses isn't coming back—and we've got to just "move on".'*

So, they approached Aaron, and we have the sad record of Aaron encouraging the people to bring their jewellery to be fashioned into an idol, before which they would proclaim, 'These are your gods, O Israel, who brought you up out of the land of Egypt' (Exodus 32:4).

Just a few chapters earlier, we read, 'Moses came and told the people all the words of the Lord and all the rules. And all the people answered with one voice and said, "All the words that the LORD has spoken we will do"' (Exodus 24:3). *'But that was then and this is now, and now we're not so sure.'*

And if people today are bothered by doubts and even tempted to think, 'What if it's all unreal, an illusion?', it is encouraging that the Bible takes account of such pressures and doubts. Aaron's story— his sad part in this episode of the golden calf—is a story about impatience, hesitation, compromise and excuses, all of which can play their part in doubt.

## Impatience

It was when the people realized that Moses had been away for more than a month that they ran out of patience. They ran out of patience in waiting for Moses, and they ran out of patience with the idea of waiting for God. They dismissed from their minds all the old stories about the unseen God who was supposed to have made everything and redeemed His people, and their sad cry was, 'Make us gods who shall go before us' (Exodus 32:1). *'Maybe Moses isn't coming back; we need to take action—we need a more visible religion.'*

It is the cry of all man-made religion that wants a god it can see and control, not to say manipulate. They said, 'Make us gods', which is a far cry from the biblical faith that begins with *God* saying, 'Let *us* make man in our image' (Genesis 1:26). Now, the Israelites had descended to the attempt to make gods—not in their own image, but in images like those of the surrounding peoples who all had their gods that they could see. 'Immortal, invisible'—*'we can't be bothered with that any longer; we want a visible god'*—and Aaron would facilitate such a project.

They were not the last generation to become impatient with God's self-revelation and make substitute gods to suit their own liking. If only they had known John 1:18: 'No one has ever seen God; the only God, who is at the Father's side, he has made him known.' Other gods are figments of human imagination; the God of the Bible is a God who exists and who makes Himself known. Our part is not to make God conform to our ideas but to conform our own thoughts, desires and ambitions to His being and His will.

There is a story about a famous person ('a celebrity', as people would say nowadays) who was 'spotted' in an ordinary shop. A bystander said, 'Wait a minute; you're ...', and then she paused as she tried to recall who it was in front of her. After a while the subject moved to ease her embarrassment and said, 'Actually I'm ...', only to be met with, 'No, no, that's not it; just give me a minute to think!' She had her own idea and nothing as simple as self-revelation was going to shift her from it![4]

Sometimes people hear or read something about God and say (or possibly just think), 'No, that's not right; give me a minute and I'll work it out.' If it is obviously better to take human beings at their word and recognize their own self-disclosure, how much more so with God.

He has made Himself known, and it is for us to respond to the God who is there and who has revealed Himself in creation; in conscience; in Scripture; and in Christ.

The apostle Paul wrote about God's self-revelation at the beginning of Romans: 'What can be known about God is plain to them, because God has shown it to them. For his invisible attributes, namely, his eternal power and divine nature, have been clearly perceived, ever since the creation of the world, in the things that have been made' (Romans 1:19–20). He went on to talk about unbelievers being 'without excuse. For although they knew God, they did not honour him as God or give thanks to him, but they became futile in their thinking… (v. 21).

John wrote about the Word becoming flesh and dwelling among us; he said, 'and we have seen his glory, glory as of the only Son from the Father, full of grace and truth' (John 1:14), and further, 'No one has ever seen God; the only God, who is at the Father's side, he has made him known' (v. 18).

There, Jesus is described as divine and the Bible's message is that if we want the reality about God, we find it in Jesus, the One in whom, according to Colossians 1:19, 'all the fullness of God was pleased to dwell'.

In all these ways—in creation, in conscience, in Scripture and in Christ—God has given us proof of His reality, so that there is no need for us to make idols, physical or mental. Indeed, not only is there no need but it would be an insult to God Himself for us human creatures to reject His own self-revelation and prefer our own ideas.

The other part of the people's request to Aaron was that he should make gods 'who shall go before us' (Exodus 32:1). They wanted a god or gods whom they could put on a cart of some kind—gods whom they could not only see but control.

It all arose from their impatience, whereas the Bible encourages us to wait on the Lord. We did not make God, we do not control God and we are to learn that 'it is good that one should wait quietly for the salvation of the Lord' (Lamentations 3:26). If there are times when faith is tested; times when we wish God would act more quickly or more obviously; times when there are trials and even temptations to turn away from the Lord, what are we to do? An old hymn tells us, 'Here let me wait with patience, wait till the night is o'er.'[5] We are to develop patience in place of impatience.

## Hesitation

When Aaron was faced with the demand, 'Make us gods', he ought to have immediately rejected any idea of human beings making gods and controlling them.

But the proverb, 'He who hesitates is lost', was true for Aaron. His hesitation allowed an element of doubt to creep into his own mind and heart and, before you could say *Mount Sinai*, he was instructing the people, '"Take off the rings of gold that are in the ears of your wives, your sons, and your daughters, and bring them to me." ... And he received the gold from their hand and fashioned it with a graving tool' (Exodus 32:2, 4) and later, in verse 24 he would say, 'I threw it into the fire, and out came this calf'!

In his heart, Aaron knew better. He knew really that such manufactured gods are no gods at all; he knew that God is the unseen God who is opposed to idolatry. But he hesitated.

It has been suggested that he was trying to defuse the situation, in the expectation that they would not go through with it—bringing all their jewellery, and so on—but, whether that was so or not, he hesitated, and he who hesitates is indeed lost.

There was impatience on the part of the people; now there is hesitation on the part of Aaron. And the Bible's message is clear: do not dilly-dally with what is wrong; do not hesitate.

There is a story of a wealthy lady who wanted to employ a chauffeur. A winding road led up to her house at the top of a hill, and at some points the road came very near to the edge of the cliff where there was a sheer drop.

Wanting to find out about the driving abilities of applicants, she asked the first, 'If you were my driver, how close could you be from the edge of the cliff without endangering us?' He said, 'I could drive within a foot of the edge and you would be safe in my hands.' She asked the same question of the second applicant and he said, 'Six inches—I can safely drive just six inches from the edge and you would be safe.' She asked the third applicant the same question and his answer was, 'If I were your driver, I would keep as far away from the edge of the cliff as possible.' The first two applicants might be skilful drivers, but the third got the job.

Hesitation, such as we see in Aaron, takes us too near the edge of the cliff; it is better to keep as far from the edge as possible. In matters of truthfulness, for example, it is better not to flirt with even little departures from the truth and, in matters of honesty, not to hesitate but to do what is honest. In relation to flirtation, it is better not to play with fire but, like Joseph, to run from it (Genesis 39:12) and, in relation to the call to witness, never to hesitate to stand up as a Christian. Sometimes we err and stray into doubt because we hesitate instead of obeying. Temptation comes, and we know what is right and what we ought to do, but we hesitate for a moment, and so we allow doubts to come in and lead us into rebellion against God.

## Compromise

In Exodus 32, the transition from verse 4 to verse 5 is rather remarkable. In verse 4, 'he received the gold from their hand and fashioned it with a graving tool and made a golden calf' and, in verse 5: 'He built an altar before it. And Aaron made a proclamation and said, "Tomorrow shall be a feast to the LORD."'

It is almost unbelievable—how could he possibly have said such a thing—unless the idol was meant to be a kind of visible *representation of* the real and living God. His words in verse 5 concerned a feast 'to the LORD'. Was it his idea that the golden calf should represent the LORD? *'Maybe the more ignorant and simple folk will actually be worshipping the calf, but we'll really be taking it as just a symbol of the unseen God.'* Could that be what was in Aaron's mind?

Whatever he had in mind (and maybe that theory would be a case of falling over backwards to defend him), the Israelites were not thinking of the Lord at all. 'They rose up early the next day and offered burnt offerings and brought peace offerings. And the people sat down to eat and drink and rose up to play' (v. 6—to 'indulge in revelry', as the NIV has it). Basically, they had an orgy.

The apostle Paul mentions the occasion in 1 Corinthians 10:6–8, when referring to the events of the exodus generally. 'These things took place as examples for us, that we might not desire evil as they did. Do not be idolaters as some of them were. As it is written, "The people sat down to eat and drink and rose up to play." We must not indulge in sexual immorality as some of them did.'

That was the outcome of the whole sad episode. Idolatry leads to immorality—as we see happening around us regularly. When people turn from the living God to worship other things—turning their backs on God—what happens to moral standards? Down they go.

And the only remedy is a return to the Lord God. Politicians and political parties try one expedient after another to improve things in our society—but the root of our problems is in the hearts of people, and it is in the hearts of people that there needs to be a change, a return to the Lord and an uncompromising commitment. We are not to seek to combine the worship of the Lord with the worship of other gods or idols. 1 Corinthians 10 goes on to say, 'You cannot drink the cup of the Lord and the cup of demons. You cannot partake of the table of the Lord and the table of demons' (v. 21).

Instead of compromising with Aaron, we should be loyal to the Lord, like Polycarp who would not listen to the voices that advised him to compromise—'I do not intend to do as you advise; For eighty and six years have I been His servant, and He has done me no wrong; how can I blaspheme my King who saved me?'

## Excuses

Aaron's story speaks of impatience, hesitation, compromise—and also, of course, of excuse-making.

Moses challenged him in Exodus 32:21, 'What did this people do to you that you have brought such a great sin upon them?'

The NIV translates Aaron's reply in verses 22–23 as the following: 'You know how prone these people are to evil. They said to me, "Make us gods who will go before us."'

And so, he explained in verse 24, 'I said to them, "Let any who have gold take it off." So, they gave it to me, and I threw it into the fire, and out came this calf.' I do not know how the translators could resist putting an exclamation mark at the end of that verse—*out came this calf* indeed!

As Adam blamed Eve and Eve blamed the serpent, Aaron tried to shift the blame from himself. He tried to blame the people, saying that they had forced him into it. Perhaps there was an implied criticism even of God, in his ridiculous, 'Out came this calf.' Was he saying, 'I didn't really fashion it; it just somehow appeared; maybe it was God who made it come out that way?'

Many people have followed Aaron's expedient, blaming God for the circumstances in which they have found themselves, the temptations that have confronted them or the kind of personality and characteristics God gave them. It is not unknown for people to claim God's guidance, even for things that clearly go against his revealed will (for example, in wrong sexual relationships when people claim that God brought them together even though they were already married to other people).

In our fallen human nature, we are prone to making excuses for ourselves—even with things which we might criticize or condemn in other people—but 'it's different in my case!' Instead of blaming our temperament, our circumstances, other people, or even the way God made us, we would do well to face up to our faults and sinfulness and turn to the Lord in repentance. 'If we say we have no sin, we deceive ourselves, and the truth is not in us. If we confess our sins, he is faithful and just to forgive us our sins and to cleanse us from all unrighteousness' (1 John 1:8–9).

Presumably Aaron did eventually repent of his wrong actions; indeed, he was the high priest, who would go into the holy of holies once a year on the day of atonement to offer sacrifices for the people's sins.

But Exodus 32 ends with God's judgement on people who persisted in rebellion, even after Moses gave them the opportunity of responding to the call, 'Who is on the LORD's side?' (Exodus 32:26). A nineteenth-century hymn-writer based a well-known hymn[6] on these words and wrote as the last verse:

> Chosen to be soldiers in an alien land,
> Chosen, called and faithful, for our Captain's band,
> In the service royal let us not grow cold;
> Let us be right loyal, noble, true and bold.
>> Master, Thou wilt keep us, by Thy grace divine,
>> Always on the Lord's side, Saviour, always Thine.

**NOTES**

1 Flew, Antony, *There Is A God*, (New York: HarperCollins, 2007). His review of Dawkins' book, mentioned in our introduction, is very interesting: www.bethinking.org/atheism/professor-

antony-flew-reviews-the-god-delusion (accessed 14/09/23).

2  Quoted from: http://www.earlychristianwritings.com/text/martyrdompolycarp-lake.html (accessed 14/09/23).

3  Although Laplace was a believer and he was really objecting to the 'God of the gaps' idea that the concept—'God'—is simply useful to fill in gaps in our knowledge. Quoted by: Coulson, C. A., *Science and Christian Belief*, (Oxford: Oxford University Press, 1955; second edition 1971), p. 41.

4  Mrs Mary Whitehouse had a similar experience when she noticed that the only other passenger in the train compartment in which she was travelling kept looking at her and then looking away again. When Mary stood up to get off at Colchester, the lady apologized and said, 'I kept wondering if you were Mrs Whitehouse. But now I can see you properly I realize you're much better-looking!' Mary Whitehouse, *Quite Contrary*, (London: Pan Macmillan, 1993), p. 160.

5  From the hymn, 'Safe in the arms of Jesus', by Frances Jane van Alstyne, 1820–1915.

6  Hymn, 'Who is on the Lord's side?' by Frances Ridley Havergal, 1836–79.

# 3 In the day of trouble

## DOUBTS ABOUT THE GOODNESS OF GOD

Another kind of doubt is doubt about God's goodness; *'Even if He is real, what kind of a being or person is He?'* If we say with the Apostles Creed, 'I believe in God', the question may be posed: *'But what kind of God do you believe in; what is He like?'*

- Is He the God of the Bible?
- Or is He just some mythical idea or a focus of society's cohesion (as emperor worship was for the Romans)?
- Could He be someone or something immanent in nature, so that in a sense we are all part of the divine?
- Worse still, what if He is a severe, tyrannical being who can only be feared—the kind of being depicted by Shakespeare when he has the blinded Gloucester say, 'As flies to wanton boys are we to th' gods—they kill us for their sport'?[1]

It is interesting—and encouraging—to find such doubts about the goodness of God *in* the Bible. We find some very straightforward questions on this subject, especially in the Psalms.

Asaph is not one of the best-known characters of the Bible but he is someone who had an important role in the worship of the Israelite people in the days of King David. The ark had been brought up to Jerusalem and the Chronicler tells of some appointments made by the king: 'He appointed some of the Levites as ministers before the ark of the Lord, to invoke, to thank, and to praise the Lord, the God of Israel. Asaph was the chief ... on that day David first appointed that thanksgiving be sung to the Lord by Asaph and his brothers' (1 Chronicles 16:4–5, 7).

Later, in connection with the dedication of the temple built by Solomon, Asaph is mentioned again as one of the Levitical singers (2 Chronicles 5:12), and twelve of the 150 Psalms bear his name (Psalms 50, 73–83); he was a worship leader and an inspired songwriter.

That being so, it is perhaps surprising to find him entertaining doubts about God's love and mercy but, as we have seen, it is one of the glories of the Bible that it does not give a bland picture of uninterrupted commitment with never the slightest shadow of any doubt.

It is a book of faith, of course, but it also records frankly that there were times when doubts bothered some of its characters, including this song-leader whose words have become the vehicle of praise for successive generations. His faith was not an untroubled faith; it was not that he lived on some higher level of faith where he was immune to any challenges to that faith.

The Puritan minister, John Flavel, referred to the difficult passages of Scripture and how serious study of them 'serves to over-power and suppress the natural atheism that is in your hearts'; Sinclair Ferguson has commented: 'Natural atheism? Flavel was a wise enough pastor to know that some true believers are afflicted with doubts about God's goodness and even his very existence.'[2]

Psalm 77 is one of Asaph's songs and when he begins verse 3 with, 'When I remember God ...' we may expect that to be followed by an expression like, 'I sing praises to your name,' or 'I rejoice at your truth and your mercy.' These are the kind of things we find expressed regularly in the Psalms, but here we read, 'When I remember God, I moan; when I meditate, my spirit faints'!

When I was a child, the first song in a popular book of choruses said, 'A little talk with Jesus makes it right, all right; In trials of every kind, praise God, I always find a little talk with Jesus make it right, all right.'³ It is good to encourage such prayerfulness in all situations of life but I suspect Asaph would have found that little chorus far too trite and, in Psalm 77, we find several things about the situation in which he experienced this time of doubt.

Firstly, we find him referring to 'the day of my trouble' (verse 2). That sets the scene for what follows as he gives voice to his doubts about God's goodness.

And giving voice to such doubts is just what the Bible tells us to do—'I cry aloud to God ... In the day of my trouble, I seek the Lord' (Psalm 77:1, 2). We are always encouraged to look up, to see beyond our own moods and feelings and take everything to the Lord in prayer, looking to the rock that is higher than we are (Psalm 61:2). But this was a time when Asaph wondered about the value of it all—all this religion, this believing in a higher power, this prayer. Was it all (to repeat C. S. Lewis' phrase) posting letters to a non-existent address?

Then he mentions sleeplessness (vv. 4–5) and a wistful remembrance of how things used to be: 'I consider the days of old, the years long ago.' During the night he longed to be able to remember his previous faith so that he could sleep easily, but the irony was that now he could not find any comfort or strength from such remembrance. Remembering the good old days only seemed to make his present predicament all the more depressing.

Is it not strange that the remembrance of past blessings can lead in opposite directions. It can bring renewed hope, but it can also lead to depression (as expressed in a once-popular song, 'Fings aint wot they used to be'). Long ago the Greek dramatist, Euripides, through a character in one of his plays, gave expression to such a hope-less view. The play deplores the barbarous cruelties of war and focuses especially on the suffering of the women of Troy. One of them (Andromache) says, 'I keep no secret deception in my heart—sweet though it be to dream—that I shall ever be happy again.'[4] It is a sad sentiment, but it is one that has been echoed by millions and millions of people who have been knocked down by one tragedy or another, which has led them to ask whether there is any justice or any meaning in life.

Here, in the realm of faith, we find something like that—Asaph looking back and thinking he will never again have the faith that once seemed such a precious and bright thing in his life and experience.

In fact, in verses 7–9 of the Psalm, we find a barrage of questions and doubts. It is like a burst from a machine-gun, one after the other—five big questions:

- 'Will the Lord spurn forever, and never again be favourable?'
- 'Has his steadfast love forever ceased?'
- 'Are his promises at an end for all time?'
- 'Has God forgotten to be gracious?'
- 'Has he in anger shut up his compassion?'

It is quite a barrage: over and over again these questions, these doubts. Was it all just imagination and delusion.

An old song says, 'Wonderful things in the Bible I see'[5]; we could also say, '*surprising things in the Bible we see*'. Asaph is a worship leader but he was in this confused condition of doubt, hovering between faith and unbelief. He had not *lost* faith—the whole Psalm is set in the context of, 'I cry aloud to God ... In the day of my trouble, I seek the Lord' (verses 1–2), but he was struggling. Even thinking about God's blessings and help in the past seemed to mock his present struggles.

And rather than just sweeping such feelings under the carpet, Asaph faced them—even though the various Psalms, attributed to him, show him to have been a strong believer and a strong encourager of others:

- One who led the people in thanksgiving to God, as in 75:1: 'We give thanks to you, O God; we give thanks, for your name is near.'
- One who was concerned that the faith should be handed on to the next generations, so that children yet unborn should learn of the Lord and revere Him. In 78:4–6 he says, 'We will ... tell to the coming generation the glorious deeds of the LORD ... which he commanded our fathers to teach to their children, that the next generation might know them, the children yet unborn, and arise and tell them to their children.'
- One who grieved over the mockery of the Lord's enemies, as in 74:10: 'How long, O God, is the foe to scoff? Is the enemy to revile your name forever?'
- One who taught about the way in which God had guided, helped and delivered His people repeatedly, even though often 'they did not believe in God and did not trust his saving power' (78:22), and often tested the Lord's patience (78:56).

- One who emphasized the fact that casual or ritual worship is useless (50:7–9).

In all these ways, Asaph had been a worthy worship leader, and yet he also had these times when he wondered about the reality of it all. And if, for us, there have been times when doubts have crept up on us, even times when we look back to the so-called good old days and that only makes the sadness sadder still, then we will sympathize with Asaph—and we will want to know what happened with him.

Psalm 77 is a psalm of two halves. In the first half, the problem is stated and then, in the second half, we are given several responses in times of doubt. They can be expressed negatively but they give us pointers to a positive response and a renewed faith.

## 1. Do not rely on your feelings

Feelings come and go. They are affected by all manner of things—the amount of sleep you have had, your digestive state, troubled relationships, even the weather—such things can affect how we feel, and feelings are not a good guide to reality.

In the latter part of the Psalm, Asaph is led to consider the facts about God's power as seen in His actions, especially in the events surrounding the exodus, and such a concentration on facts rather than feelings is one antidote to doubt. It has been expressed, 'As a gauge of spirituality they (our feelings) are about as reliable as a sundial at midnight.'[6]

Of course, there is a balance to be struck. Christianity *does* involve the emotions, the feelings. It is not a cold and barren thing in which we just believe certain truths in our heads and that is all. We are told to love the Lord with all our heart as well as with all our mind and soul (Matthew 22:37), and indeed the Psalms are full of expressions of heart-*felt* faith and worship.

Sometimes as believers we may have an overwhelming sense of the greatness and grace of God. It is the kind of thing we find in the New Testament. To take one example, we find Paul wrestling with the issues of divine sovereignty and human free-will in *Romans*. It is not always easy to follow (even Peter wrote about how there are some things in Paul's writings that are 'hard to understand'—2 Peter 3:16). But, after grappling with deep questions, Paul bursts out with, 'Oh, the depth of the riches and wisdom and knowledge of God! How unsearchable are his judgements and how inscrutable his ways!' (Romans 11:33).

It is inevitable that the emotions should be involved. We are human beings, after all, not automatons or robots.

At the same time, however, feelings are not necessarily to be relied on, and Asaph needed something more solid than his emotions to overcome his doubts. 'I will remember the deeds of the LORD; yes, I will remember your wonders of old ... You are the God who works wonders; you have made known your might among the peoples' (Psalm 77:11, 14).

Faith is based on the nature of God Himself and the way in which He has acted, supremely in sending His Son that whoever believes in Him should not perish but have everlasting life (John 3:16).

An old hymn (which was quoted earlier) says,

> 'Twixt gleams of joy and clouds of doubt our feelings come and go;
> Our best estate is tossed about in ceaseless ebb and flow.
> No mood of feeling, form of thought, is constant for a day;
> But Thou, O Lord, Thou changest not; the same Thou art always.[7]

The hymn continues:

> Let me no more my comfort draw from my frail hold of Thee;
> In this alone rejoice with awe—Thy mighty grasp of me.

## 2. Learn from the past

As we have seen, Psalm 77 goes on to refer to the event, which was to the people of Israel what the message of the cross and the empty tomb is to Christians. Asaph refers to their deliverance from Egyptian captivity and the ensuing events, bringing the Hebrews through the waters to their own promised land: 'Your way was through the sea, your path through the great waters; yet your footprints were unseen' (verse 19). No one could actually see God leading His people, yet the evidence of His guidance and His presence was unmistakeable.

For us, the psalm is part (not only of the Old Testament but) of the whole Bible and ever since the incarnation of the Son of God and the atonement made through the cross of Christ, the words are even more significant: 'You with your arm redeemed your people' (v. 15).

As Peter would write to believers in his day:

> You were ransomed from the futile ways inherited from your forefathers, not with perishable things such as silver or gold, but with the precious blood of Christ, like that of a lamb without blemish or spot. He was foreknown before the foundation of the world but was made manifest in the last times for the sake of you who through him are believers in God, who raised him from the dead and gave him glory, so that your faith and hope are in God (1 Peter 1:18–21)—*not in your own feelings or moods but in God.*

Peter says it is through Christ that we believe in God:

- the Lord who came to the world as a human being
- the Lord who was tested and temped in every way as we are, though without sinning
- the Lord who spoke such marvellous words—the Sermon on the Mount, the parables, etc.
- the Lord who broke barriers—having time for Zacchaeus, the woman by the well and others
- the Lord who could do amazing things, like feeding 5000 people with five loaves and two fish
- the Lord who would die on the cross to pay the penalty of sin and redeem His people
- the Lord who would burst from the tomb and who promised to come again.

The last verse of Psalm 77 says, 'You led your people like a flock by the hand of Moses and Aaron'—these men who at times had their doubts but who became great leaders of the people.

And the word about shepherding surely brings to mind the saying of Jesus about being the Good Shepherd who would give His life for the sheep (John 10:11). He led His people like a flock by the hand of Someone greater than Moses or Aaron or any other human leader.

The answer to our doubts is to be found in going back again and again to Calvary, in the spirit of Isaac Watts' great hymn (which Matthew Arnold called the greatest hymn in the English language) to 'survey the wondrous cross on which the Prince of Glory died; Love so amazing, so divine, demands my soul, my life, my all.'[8]

**3. Resist the temptation to leave off prayer and worship for now**

This is another lesson of Psalm 77. Asaph may have been struggling; in Psalm 73 he begins with the orthodox statement of faith, 'Truly God is good to Israel'. However, that is followed by the word 'but' in v. 2. He wrote, 'My feet had almost stumbled, my steps had nearly slipped'. He wondered whether it was all in vain that he had kept his heart clean and washed his hands in innocence (73:13)—but it is *to God* that such sentiments are addressed. Instead of turning away from Him with all his queries and doubts, he turns *to* the Lord.

Turning away from Him in such times would be like having toothache and thinking, '*But I had better stay away from dentists until my teeth are in a better condition.*' Obviously, the thing to do if you have toothache is to go to the dentist, and if we have doubts and questions, it is good to follow Asaph's example, as expressed in Psalm 73:16–17: 'When I thought how to understand this, it seemed to me a wearisome task, until I went into the sanctuary of God.' Clearly, it was not the mere act of entering the building that made the difference but it was when he persisted in worship and prayer that light came to him.

Sadly, this is counter to what many people do or are tempted to do. Often people who are troubled by doubts and questions turn *away* from the Lord but the best thing is, even in such a time (perhaps especially in such a time), to turn *to* Him.

God, we might say, is big enough to contain all our doubts and questions; He is loving enough to receive us as we come—as the famous hymn says:

Just as I am, though tossed about
With many a conflict, many a doubt,
Fightings and fears within, without,
O Lamb of God, I come.[9]

We do not have to wait until we know all the answers and have all our queries sorted out; even if there are pieces of the jigsaw not yet in place, that need not keep us away from faith. We can take everything—including such conflicts and doubts—to Him. It may be tempting to neglect prayer and worship in the time of trial but Asaph teaches us to take everything to the Lord in prayer.

It is said that during the East African Revival in the 1920s and 1930s, when some converts lived in cramped houses, they would make their way each day to their own clearing in the bush to pray and give thanks. Gradually a path would be worn down, so that if anyone neglected their times of prayer and worship, it would become evident; a fellow believer would say, 'There's grass on your path, brother.'

Asaph would not allow grass to grow over his path. He was the chief praise-leader appointed by King David, but his faith was not an easy or superficial thing. It was tested by doubt: 'Has his steadfast love for ever ceased? Are his promises at an end for all time?' That is what he was tempted to think, but in his response, he teaches us not to rely on feelings, not to forget the deeds of the Lord and not to neglect prayer.

**NOTES**

1  *King Lear*, 111, iv, 36

2  Ferguson, Sinclair B., *Some Pastors and Teachers* (Edinburgh: Banner of Truth 2017), p. 319.

3  *C.S.S.M. Choruses* (London: C.S.S.M., 1959) No. 1.

4  In the stage performance of *The Trojan Women* at the Edinburgh International Festival, 1966.

5  From the hymn, 'I am so glad that our Father in heav'n', by Philip Paul Bliss (1838-1876).

6  Dunn, R., *Don't Just Sit There—Have Faith*, (Milton Keynes: Paternoster, 2000), p. 102.

7  Hymn by John Campbell Shairp, 1819–85.

8  Hymn by Isaac Watts, 1674–1748.

9  Hymn by Charlotte Elliott, 1789–1871.

# 4 Too good to be true?

## DOUBTS ABOUT THE TRUSTWORTHINESS OF GOD

The Bible is full of great and wonderful promises for believers. For example, Isaiah 26:3 says, 'You keep him in perfect peace whose mind is stayed on you, because he trusts in you,' and Jude 24 promises, '[He] is able to keep you from stumbling.' But what about the times when a little voice of doubt whispers in our ear, '*What if it's all just a nice story? What if we've been conned into believing a myth? What if there isn't any reality behind it all?*' That is what we are concerned with in this chapter—is it all too good to be true?

*God makes me laugh* might have been the title for this chapter—not because it is about the gift of humour but because it refers, as we shall see, to two people who laughed at the promise which God gave them. It seemed so unlikely, so ridiculous really, that they could not help laughing at the promise that the aged Abraham's aged wife, Sarah, would give birth to a son.

It really is not surprising that Abraham and Sarah should find God's promise incredible. And if these stalwarts of faith could have such gloomy moments, it is not surprising if others too experience times when things, that once seemed simple, begin to look improbable.

Sometimes in churches people sing, 'Trust and obey for there's no other way to be happy in Jesus but to trust and obey,'[1] but that hymn also has a verse that says, 'Not a doubt nor a fear ... can abide while we trust and obey.' If we balk at such a statement, we are in good company and, in this chapter, we consider the experience of someone who is held up in the Bible as a great example of faith.

Abraham and Sarah might have balked at that verse. They sought to trust in the Lord and obey His call, but for them that did not mean the end of all doubts.

Their experience may be an encouragement to others who find that trusting and obeying does not automatically dispel all doubts once and for ever. It is a very good thing to follow the way of the old hymn that bids us count our blessings[2] in all the circumstances of life but, 'Count your many blessings—every doubt will fly,' may not always be immediately true.

In Genesis 17:15–21, we read about God promising that Abraham's wife Sarah would have a baby:

> 'I will bless her, and moreover, I will give you a son by her. I will bless her, and she shall become nations; kings of peoples shall come from her.' Then Abraham fell on his face and laughed and said to himself, 'Shall a child be born to a man who a hundred years old? Shall Sarah, who is ninety years old, bear a child?' ... God said, '... Sarah your wife shall bear you a son and you shall call his name Isaac ... I will establish my covenant with Isaac, whom Sarah shall bear to you at this time next year'.

Genesis 18:13–14 tells of Sarah also laughing at the thought and then we have the Lord's response, 'Why did Sarah laugh and say, "Shall I indeed bear a child, now that I am old?" Is anything too hard for the LORD?' The name Isaac is derived from the word for laughter and the story is that of the overcoming of Abraham and Sarah's doubts concerning the seemingly unlikely promise of God.

Genesis tells us about the testimony and then the testing of Abraham's faith.

### The testimony of Abraham's faith

Firstly, there is the statement in Genesis 15:6: 'He believed the LORD, and he counted it to him as righteousness.' That phrase is quoted no less than four times in the New Testament:

- Romans 4:3—'What does the Scripture say? "Abraham believed God, and it was counted to him as righteousness."'
- Romans 4:20–22—'He grew strong in his faith as he gave glory to God, fully convinced that God was able to do what he had promised. That is why his faith was "counted to him as righteousness".'
- Galatians 3:6–9—'Abraham "believed God, and it was counted to him as righteousness". Know then that it is those of faith who are the sons of Abraham. And the Scripture, foreseeing that God would justify the Gentiles by faith, preached the gospel beforehand to Abraham, saying, "In you shall all the nations be blessed." So then, those who are of faith are blessed along with Abraham, the man of faith.'
- James 2:21–23—'Was not Abraham our father justified by works when he offered up his son Isaac on the altar? You see that faith was active along with his works, and faith was completed by his works; and the Scripture was fulfilled that says, "Abraham believed God, and it was counted to him as righteousness".'

The words, spoken first in Genesis 15:6, come from Abraham's initial reaction to the promise of a son, which was obviously the key to the fulfilment of God's earlier promise (Genesis 12) of a land and countless descendants; you cannot have many descendants unless you have one child to start with. In chapter 15, the promise was repeated and Abraham believed it. Romans 4:18 says, 'In hope he believed against hope, that he should become the father of many nations, as he had been told,' but what we find in Genesis 17 is that this faith and hope did not come without a struggle. There were times when Abraham, and Sarah also, found it hard to believe.

### The testing of Abraham's faith

The other Biblical illustration of Abraham as 'the man of faith' (Galatians 3:9), is the story recorded in Genesis 22 when his trust in God was tested on Mount Moriah.

Isaac had been born and we can imagine people looking at the baby and saying to the elderly couple, 'What a lovely grandchild you have,' before Abraham or Sarah would explain, 'No, this is our son, this is Isaac, this is the fulfilment of the promise God made to us.'

But later, we read of God's instruction to take Isaac to the land of Moriah 'and offer him there as a burnt offering on one of the mountains of which I shall tell you' (Genesis 22:2). It must have seemed absurd. Was not Isaac the long-awaited fulfilment of the promise and how could it be that God would require him to be sacrificed?

Of course, God did not require him to be sacrificed, but he was testing Abraham's faith: did he trust God enough to sacrifice everything that was involved in the promises of God? Abraham believed in God, but did he have enough faith to really trust Him? Everything was bound up in this child; this was the guarantee of descendants as numerous as the grains of sand on the seashore (Genesis 22:17).

Without going into the detail of the story, it turns out that, although God did not require the sacrifice of Isaac, Abraham's faith did hold firm through it all. As Os Guinness has put it, 'It was because he knew who God was that he knew he could trust God in the dark. More precisely still, it was because he was not in the dark about God that he could walk in the dark about Isaac. In terms of his immediate situation, he did not know why, but in terms of the ultimate context of his life *he knew why he trusted God who knew why*.'[3]

The hymn, quoted at the start of this chapter, takes the story as a challenge to trust God absolutely and in every aspect of our lives; it says, 'But we never can prove the delights of His love until all on the altar we lay.'

These are probably the two best-known incidents in the life of Abraham and, in both, he is seen as a great example of complete trust.

### Is God trustworthy?

But in this chapter, we are concerned with what happened in between these two incidents. The Bible is honest in telling of this time when Abraham found it hard to believe; he had doubts about God's ability to fulfil His promises. It is not that he doubted God's existence, or had the vague faith of those who talk lightly about '*something up there*'—but is He a God to be trusted and can He indeed fulfil His promises?

Even Abraham, this great man of faith, laughed and said to himself, 'Shall a child be born to a man who is a hundred years old?'

He was not going to be carried away into the realm of the impossible; he was, after all, a realist and not a dreamer.

The following chapter tells of three men who visited him at Mamre and reiterated the promise of a child for Sarah, that provoked her incredulous laughter, which in turn provoked the Lord's question, 'Is anything too hard for the LORD?'

It is a question for today also. We can easily come to doubt the ability of God and become people of little faith (Matthew 14:31). The late David Watson told of an emergency meeting of church leaders that was called because of a crisis in the congregation. The chairman opened the meeting in prayer, addressing God as the Almighty and Eternal God, whose grace is sufficient for all things and to whom nothing is impossible. Then he introduced the business of the meeting and said, 'Gentlemen, the situation in this church is hopeless and nothing can be done about it!'[4]

Few of us would fall into such a trap (hopefully!) but doubt can easily characterize the faith in our hearts and the prayers on our lips. We pray for the turning of the tide in our nation, for the reversal of the decline of the church, for power to overcome a recurring temptation, for the conversion of a friend—and we can easily become like the believers who were praying for the imprisoned Peter but, when told that he was at the door, they said to the messenger, 'You are out of your mind!' (Acts 12:15). They could not believe that the very thing for which they had been praying had actually happened!

It may be something of an encouragement to know that even Abraham could doubt God's ability to fulfil His promises and, through his story, there is the challenge for us to trust God more fully.

For him, faith was not an easy thing. It also reminds us of the principle that doubt is not the opposite of faith. The opposite of faith is unbelief; doubt is that experience which Romans 4:20 (ESV) describes as 'wavering'. Romans emphasizes that Abraham did not fall into unbelief. It is the devil who would use doubt to lead people into unbelief, but Abraham came through the time of doubt to a convinced faith that nothing is too hard for God.

However, the Biblical account of Abraham and his faith does tell of a wrong action and a wrong attitude.

## A wrong action

The wrong action is described in Genesis 16 which begins with the matter-of-fact statement, 'Now Sarai, Abram's wife, had borne him no children.'

The whole covenant depended on Abraham having children, or at least a child. And that chapter tells of Sarai suggesting to Abraham that God seemed to be needing a little help in the fulfilment of His promise. After all, she might have said, the original promise was that *Abraham* would have a son; it did not at the outset say anything about Sarah and—no doubt after much agonizing about the idea— she came up with the suggestion that it might be by a surrogate, her servant Hagar, that the promise would be fulfilled.

Abraham agreed to this stratagem and in due time Ishmael was born. So it was that doubt about God's ability to fulfil His Word that led them into trying to force God's hand. They did not doubt God's existence, but their loss of patience led them to doubt whether God was able to do what He had promised.

We possibly should not judge this by the fuller revelation that we have in the completed Word of God. But it was a wrong action; God does not need our help to make His promises come true. He may choose to work through human agency, but He is not dependent on us.

And when, in chapter 17, the promise is repeated, it is made very specific. It would be through *Sarah* that the promise would be fulfilled: 'I will bless her, and moreover, I will give you a son *by her*' (v.16).

Patience is a quality we need to learn. Much later it would be written (in the AKJV of Habakkuk 2:3), 'Though it [the vision] tarry, wait for it.' By nature, we are inclined to want to rush God—to make things happen more quickly instead of waiting for Him to fulfil His Word in His own way and in His own time. There may be times when we need to get up and get on with whatever God calls us to do, but patience is part of the fruit of the Spirit and one part of the remedy for doubts about God's ability to fulfil His promises.

### A wrong attitude

If the plan for Abraham to father a child by Hagar was the wrong action, it also betrays a wrong attitude. We have noted that both Abraham and Sarah laughed at God's promise that Sarah would bear a son.

There are different kinds of laughter, ranging from honest-to-goodness laughter, which is one of God's creation gifts, to the laughter of scorn and derision. Of the first, Proverbs 17:22 says (in its AKJV form), 'A merry heart doeth good like a medicine,' and that is different from the cynical laughter of scorn, such as is illustrated in the New Testament story of the raising of Jairus' daughter. Luke (who was a doctor) tells us that when Jesus said the girl was '"not dead but sleeping," … They laughed at him, knowing that she was dead' (Luke 8:52–53). There is the attitude of scorn; in the name of realism, they simply *knew* that she was dead and therefore they could laugh at Jesus.

Abraham and Sarah both laughed at the promise. They needed to take seriously the ability of God to fulfil His promises; they needed patience and a renewed trust in God's Word. Genesis 18:13–14 says that the LORD spoke again to Abraham: 'Why did Sarah laugh … Is anything too hard for the LORD?'

We have the great privilege, which Abraham and Sarah did not have, of having the whole written Word of God in our hands, and it is in this book that there lies the remedy for this kind of doubt. Other books may amuse, entertain and inform, but this book is in a class of its own because 'The Spirit breathes upon the Word and brings the truth to sight'[5] and the answer to doubts about God's ability to fulfil His promises lies in the book.

If C. S. Lewis' *The Screwtape Letters* was writing on the subject, he might well advise his client to forget about the Bible *meantime*, perhaps until these doubts have passed (*you can come back to such matters if and when your doubts and questions have been satisfactorily answered*)—but the very opposite is our real need: to get back to the Word of God so that we hear Him speaking to us again.

In the time of doubt, it may seem appropriate to 'go into neutral'—leave off praying, stay away from worship services, etc—but it is the very time to turn, not away from the Lord, but to Him.

The Bible itself promises that if we seek Him with all our hearts, He will be found by us. The context of these words could have been applied to Abraham and Sarah: 'I know the plans I have for you, declares the LORD, plans for welfare and not for evil, to give you a future and a hope.' Then comes the promise, 'You will seek me and find me, when you seek me with all your heart' (Jeremiah 29:11, 13).

So it is, that we see in Abraham (*even* Abraham) a wrong action and a wrong attitude, and we learn about the need for patience and a renewed hearing of God's Word.

### 'Is anything too hard for the LORD?'

Perhaps it is an encouragement that this great Biblical exemplar of faith came to that faith through testing.

In the New Testament, James took up that subject: 'The testing of your faith produces steadfastness.' He went on, 'And let steadfastness have its full effect, that you may be perfect and complete, lacking in nothing. If any of you lacks wisdom, let him ask God, who gives generously to all without reproach, and it will be given him' (James 1:3–5).

James also referred to doubt: 'Let him ask in faith, with no doubting, for the one who doubts is like a wave of the sea that is driven and tossed by the wind' (v. 6). The image suggests the instability that comes from doubting God's Word (Adam and Eve) and doubting God's promises (Abraham and Sarah).

In due time God did fulfil His promise: Isaac was born and the line of promise was continued.

At a later time, He would lead His people out of Egyptian slavery in the great Exodus that looked impossible—what power was there that could take on Pharaoh and the might of Egypt? We referred to the power that could even raise Jairus' daughter from the dead, after people had laughed at Jesus. This is the God who would also turn around the life of Saul of Tarsus, in another event that looked so unlikely and yet it happened, so that Paul became the great missionary to the gentiles.

The line of Abraham, Isaac and Jacob led on through the centuries until 'the fullness of time had come (and) God sent forth his Son, born of woman, born under the law, to redeem those who were under the law, so that we might receive adoption as sons' (Galatians 4:4–5).

Is anything too hard for God? We are challenged to stop thinking that some things are impossible for Him—whether it is the healing of someone who is ill, the conversion of someone who has no time for the things of God, the revival and renewal of the church, or the turning around of our society from its slide into moral decadence and lunacy. It may be the power to overcome some besetting temptation or the ability to come through some trying time of persecution, illness, anxiety or uncertainty.

Far from it all being too good to be true, it is too true to be doubted.

### NOTES

1 Hymn by John H. Sammis, 1846–1919.
2 Hymn by Johnson Oatman, Jr., 1856–1922.
3 Guiness, Os, *Doubt*, (Berkhamstead: Lion, 1976), p. 87. Guinness also wrote, 'As we go on in our faith, we may be led into areas "beyond reason", but what we mean by this is beyond humanly discernible reasons and not in any sense against reason' (p. 89).
4 Watson, David C. K., *God's Freedom Fighters*, (Movement Books, 1972), p. 86f.
5 Quoting the hymn by William Cowper, 1731–1800.

# 5 What is it all about?

## DOUBTS ABOUT THE MEANING OF LIFE

We have considered doubts about God's Word, God's reality, God's goodness and God's trustworthiness. Another kind of doubt is doubt about whether life has any meaning at all. The actor, Marlon Brando, said, 'Life is a mystery and it is an unsolvable one. You just simply live it through and as you draw your last breath you say, "What was that all about?"'[1] Was he right? Is there any meaning or real significance to our existence?

That question is the theme of the Old Testament book of Ecclesiastes. The Hebrew name of the author, Qoheleth, is sometimes translated as, 'The Preacher'; the ESV Student Study Bible suggests 'Collector' and another option could be 'The Philosopher' as he does indeed get into fundamental questions about reality and the meaning of things. It has traditionally been assumed that Solomon was the author and, in this chapter, we shall go with that assumption.

In the book, Solomon faces up to this question of whether our lives have any meaning or whether everything is just 'vanity'. That is the force of the first words of the book (1:2): 'Vanity of vanities! All is vanity.' The theme is that if we allow doubt to lead us on to unbelief—the rejection of faith in God—then life becomes meaningless; conversely it is when we actually trust in Him that we find purpose and meaning.

Ecclesiastes is a book with a powerful relevance for our times. There is a well-justified concern about the growth in the number of people who see so little point in living that they commit suicide. Suicide accounts for one in five deaths among young people, especially males in the 35–45 age group. Statistics for 2018 say that, in Scotland, there were 784 suicides, which represents a 15% increase over the previous year.

And presumably there are many more who would never go to that extreme, but who see no purpose in life.

There are no easy answers to such problems; and of course, it is also true that, in the case of mental illness and clinical depression, people of faith can be affected as much as anyone. But there can be little doubt that a sense of purpose which comes from trusting in the Lord would make such self-destruction a much less likely thing.

The writer of Ecclesiastes clearly 'had it all'. In chapter 2, he lists his achievements: he had houses (plural), vineyards, gardens and parks, pools from which to water a forest of trees. He had many slaves, more herds and flocks than anyone before him and plenty of money.

And his conclusion? 'Then I considered all that my hands had done … and behold … there was nothing to be gained under the sun' (Ecclesiastes 2:11). It anticipates the word of Someone greater than Solomon who would ask what profit there would be in gaining the whole world if you lose your soul (Luke 9:25).

Ecclesiastes packs a powerful punch for our advanced and sophisticated society, with blessings which previous generations could never have imagined. People seek fulfilment through entertainment ('amusing ourselves to death', as Neil Postman put it[2]), through money and possessions (or the desire for wealth: every week Britons spend £82,000,000 on lottery tickets, despite the fact that 99.99% of participants lose), through physical pleasure, through fame or recognition, and in other ways.

And all the time, the Bible tells us that our hearts will always be restless and unfulfilled until they find rest in the God who made us, who sent His Son to die for us and who reminds us that a day lies ahead when we must all appear before Him to give an account of ourselves.

This book (*Dealing With Doubt*) is about seeking *answers* to doubt, but ironically Ecclesiastes might be said to be a book that *raises* doubts.

The Bible generally seeks to deal with doubts; for example, the psalmist of Psalm 42 says to himself, 'Why are you cast down, O my soul, and why are you in turmoil within me? Hope in God; for I shall again praise him, my salvation and my God' (Psalm 42:5–6).

The Bible seeks to answer doubt and encourage faith. But Ecclesiastes is different, in that it actually seeks to raise doubts where perhaps there were not any before. Beforehand, people were going along cheerfully without any thought about ultimate or eternal things, and along comes Ecclesiastes with its challenging and even disturbing question—what is life all about?

For many people, much of life consists of the attempt to keep such questions at bay and avoid thinking about them. Albert Einstein even said, 'To ponder interminably over the reason for one's existence or the meaning of life in general seems to me, from an objective point of view, to be sheer folly.'[3] But this is like trying to sink a cork in water—it keeps bobbing up again.

Ecclesiastes expresses the view that life without God ('under the sun') is meaningless and the book is really a critique of secularism. It raises doubt, but only in order to lead people to faith, to the attitude that is summed up at the end of Ecclesiastes: 'The end of the matter; all has been heard. Fear God and keep his commandments, for this is the whole duty of man' (12:13).

That is his conclusion, the end-result of all the exposure of the barrenness of a purely 'this-worldly' way. Its thrust is summed up in the hymn, 'O grant us light':

> O grant us light, that we may learn
> How dead is life from Thee apart;
> How sure is joy for all who turn
> To Thee an undivided heart.[4]

## 'Under the sun'

One of the features of Ecclesiastes is the recurring phrase, 'under the sun'. The book drives home the message that all is vanity *if* life is lived merely 'under the sun'. Confine everything to this material and physical world, and things just will not 'add up'.

A striking testimony, which resonates with the theme of Ecclesiastes, comes from the experience of Jonathan Aitken, who was a minister of state in the government of the United Kingdom but who committed perjury, for which he was convicted and imprisoned. He became a committed Christian and looked back in this way:

> At the time that I moved to the forefront of British politics, I was one of those people who call themselves a Christian without actually being one. Externally I could almost be described as a pillar of the Church of England, for I had grown up loving its music as a school, village and occasional cathedral choirboy. As a family we went to church virtually every Sunday throughout the 1980s and 1990s.... Yet for all this outward piety, I do not think that I had fully appreciated that true religion is a predominantly internal activity.[5]

As he progressed in his political career, he wrote:

> In my heart of hearts, I was aware that something was going seriously wrong with my hitherto vaulting ambition and my appetite for power. What that something was, I did not know. All I could tell was that the more my career prospered on the surface, the more my deeper feelings were signalling an emptiness and lack of fulfilment within.... Gnawing away inside me was a problem I could not describe, except by giving it psychobabble labels such as 'lack of inner peace', 'emptiness of feeling', 'hollowness of spirit' or more simply, 'something missing'. It was as though, after spending a lifetime wanting to climb a particular mountain, I had unexpectedly reached the final approach only to discover that there was nothing there worth the effort of the ascent.... As far as any external eye could see, I was a fulfilled and happy politician whose star was rising and whose cup was full. Against a background of family contentment and financial security, I was riding high on the crest of an exciting career wave, which in a sea of tired Cabinet colleagues seemed likely to take me onwards and upwards to still more powerful positions. But for what purpose.[6]

Aitken went on to find meaning and purpose through his Christian conversion, but that last question, 'for what purpose?' expresses well the theme of Ecclesiastes. Einstein may say that it is folly to 'ponder interminably over the reasons for one's own existence or the meaning of life in general' but the Bible says it is folly to *neglect* the big issues: where did we come from, why are we here and where are we going?

Ecclesiastes begins with the rather gloomy note, 'Vanity of vanities, says the Preacher, vanity of vanities! All is vanity' (1:2), and we find the same at the end: 'Vanity of vanities, says the Preacher; all is vanity' (12:8). And in between these two statements about meaninglessness, Solomon gives something of his own testimony about various things which led him to the conclusion that life without God is meaningless and only with Him is real peace, contentment and meaning found.

He refers to four things which, together, led him to this conclusion. They are factors to contemplate in our contemporary world also.

### a) The inability of worldly things to satisfy the quest for meaning

The writer of the book seemed to have everything going for him in terms of wealth, power and pleasure:

- As to wealth: Ecclesiastes 2:4–5 says, 'I made great works. I built houses and planted vineyards for myself. I made myself gardens and parks, and planted in them all kinds of fruit trees.' He had slaves and 'great possessions of herds and flocks, more than any who had been before me in Jerusalem. I ... gathered for myself silver and gold and the treasure of kings and provinces' (vv. 7–8). This is someone who lacked nothing.

  But did his wealth bring him peace of mind? In 2:11 he confesses, 'I considered all that my hands had done and the toil I had expended in doing it, and behold, all was vanity and a striving after wind, and there was nothing to be gained under the sun.'

  The testimony of Jonathan Aitken reminds us that this is not simply a story from long ago. The theme is just as relevant today as it was then, even if the outward expressions of wealth and achievement are different. People can have everything money can buy and still be unfulfilled and empty.

No amount of material wealth can satisfy the deepest needs or answer the deepest questions of the human heart.

- As for power, Solomon was king in Jerusalem. Nobody was more powerful and, of course, we are not referring to a constitutional monarchy such as we enjoy in the United Kingdom. Then, kings had enormous personal power. Yet, 'Even in the night his heart does not rest. This also is vanity' (v. 23)—such was his testimony. That too we have seen in the case of Jonathan Aitken.
- And pleasure? 2:1 says, 'I said in my heart, "Come now, I will test you with pleasure; enjoy yourself."' He says, 'Whatever my eyes desired I did not keep from them' (2:10), but such pleasure did not bring him the peace or joy he sought or answer his doubts about the purpose and value of life.

## b) The inevitability of death

The writer was aware also of the shortness of life in this world: 'What happens to the children of man and what happens to the beasts is the same; as one dies, so dies the other. They all have the same breath, and man has no advantage over the beasts, for all is vanity' (3:19). And he echoes the refrain heard often at funeral services: 'All are from the dust, and to dust all return' (3:20). Such is the gloomy outlook; what if this is all that can be said about our lives?

A few years ago, an online article referred to a particular week of the year which had been designated as Dying Awareness Week—a campaign designed to get people talking and thinking more about death. The writer quoted a *Guardian* article which noted, 'Funerals are difficult for everyone, but young people can find them particularly disconcerting. I was standing at the graveside as the coffin of a 21-year-old whose life had been cut short by a particularly vigorous cancer, was lowered. Very quietly, almost under her breath, one of her friends whispered, "Is this it? Is this all there is?"[7] That is a contemporary equivalent of an inscription found on some Roman tombstones: 'NF F NS NC'—standing for, *Non fui, fui, non sum, non curo.* That might be better left in Latin because it means, 'I was not, I was, I am not, I care not.'

If there are times when believers have doubts about whether there is anything after this life, Ecclesiastes invites people to doubt such doubts, especially in light of the inevitability of death and the hopelessness of a purely this-worldly outlook.

And of course, elsewhere the Bible reminds us that we must all die and appear before our Maker (Hebrews 9:27). Death is inevitable and if we want to make sense of life, we have to somehow make sense of death; the one certainty of our existence.

## c) The injustices of the world

Solomon felt, as many another has felt, that there are things which happen in the world that make us wonder about whether there is any purpose in what takes place. Ecclesiastes 3:16 again uses the expression, 'under the sun' and says, 'I saw under the sun that in the place of justice, even there was wickedness, and in the place of righteousness, even there was wickedness.'

Ecclesiastes 4:1 rubs in the point: 'I saw all the oppressions that are done under the sun. And behold, the tears of the oppressed, and they had no one to comfort them! On the side of their oppressors there was power, and there was no one to comfort them.'

The gloom gets even deeper in verses 2–3 that follow: 'I thought the dead who are already dead more fortunate than the living who are still alive. But better than both is he who has not yet been and has not seen the evil deeds that are done under the sun.'

Some people seek comfort in the thought of extinction at death. The broadcaster, Joan Bakewell, asked the then Poet Laureate, Andrew Motion, what he thought death is. He answered, 'Nothing. The only thing that keeps me awake sweating at night is the idea that there might be something. I just want to go out like a light.'[8]

The Polish Nobel-prize-winning poet, Czeslaw Milosz, wrote an essay entitled, 'The Discreet Charms of Nihilism', in which he reflects on Marx's famous charge that religion is the opiate of the people. Milosz wrote, 'A true opium of the people is a belief in nothingness after death—the huge solace of thinking that our betrayals, greed, cowardice, murders are not going to be judged.'[9]

This would be a very welcome notion for (say) a serial murderer or rapist—the idea of 'getting away with it'. A sense of outrage at such a possibility may not be an *argument* for the reality of God and judgement, but it does speak of a deeply embedded sense of justice in the human heart which, according to Christian belief, has been planted there by a righteous Creator whose ways are just and true (Revelation 15:3) and whose Word warns us not to presume on His patience. That patience is meant to lead us to repentance—otherwise, as Paul says, we are storing up wrath for ourselves on the day of wrath when God's righteous judgement will be revealed' (Romans 2:4–5).

For Solomon, the injustices of this world provide a reason to doubt our doubts about life and death.

## d) The insufficiency of human wisdom to solve the problem

The other factor that led to Solomon's challenge to doubt is the simple fact that human intelligence, which can achieve so much, cannot bring a sense of meaning and an answer to doubt. His testimony is, 'I applied my heart to seek and to search out by wisdom all that is done under heaven … and behold, all is vanity and a striving after wind' (1:13–14).

Our God-given human ingenuity has achieved wonderful things, especially in an age when we see technological and scientific advances that would have been incredible to past generations. But that human cleverness cannot give an answer to the most basic of questions; we can put people on the moon and yet we cannot solve the problems of *this* world. The simple truth is 'man cannot find out the work that is done under the sun. However much man may toil in seeking, he will not find it out. Even though a wise man claims to know, he cannot find it out' (8:17).

In Jonathan Aitken's testimony, he wrote of a time when he had faced up to his own sin and the crime of perjury, plus the prospect of trial and imprisonment; yet he spoke of having accepted Christ into his heart as his Lord and God. Then, he wrote that, if there were days of doubt and faltering, 'something extraordinary happened or someone remarkable appeared by my side to keep me going.'

In a series of rhetorical questions, he asked:

> Why on earth should I keep getting letters day after day, often from virtual or total strangers, telling me they were remembering me in their prayers? Why on earth should a disparate collection of acquaintances have grappled their souls to mine in an intimate and prayerful friendship? … Why on earth should my chronic asthma

suddenly recover to the point of near-normal breathing after an embarrassing (at first) laying on of hands ... Why on earth should my relationships with my children, my sister and my mother have blossomed into so much happiness at a time when all the outside world could see was a landscape of unhappiness?

Such were his questions, and then:

The answers were beyond me until I realized that I was asking the wrong questions by prefacing them with the phrase, 'Why on earth ...' For the explanations were not earthly, even though the results of them were often down to earth. The mysterious and loving presence of God was there too.[10]

This is an interesting contemporary parallel to what Solomon wrote: 'man cannot find out the work that is done under the sun. However much man may toil in seeking it, he will not find it out. Even though a wise man claims to know, he cannot find it out' (8:17).

If this is so, if some things are simply beyond our understanding, does this mean that there is no hope of anyone ever finding the key to life and its meaning?

## A revelation of purpose

The answer is found in the bottom-line fact that Ecclesiastes is a book of the Bible, and the Bible is God's revelation to humankind. It was not produced 'by the will of man, but men spoke from God as they were carried along by the Holy Spirit' (2 Peter 1:21). Peter was still Peter, Matthew was still Matthew, Jeremiah was still Jeremiah, each writing with his own style and in his own context, but behind all of that was the inspiration of God's Spirit.

Human wisdom consists in paying heed to that which God has made known. He has spoken 'at many times and in many ways ... (and) in these last days, he has spoken to us by his Son, whom he appointed the heir of all things, through whom also he created the world' (Hebrews 1:1–2).

It is a commonplace piece of advice that, when we acquire a new device or machine, the best course of action is to follow the maker's instructions. The person or company who made the object is best placed to advise about how to use it and get the best from it.

In the highest realm of all, how foolish would it be to adopt the attitude of the person who says, 'If all else fails, follow the instructions' (or, in the words of comedian Tim Taylor on a postcard I received, 'Real men don't use instructions; they are only the manufacturer's opinion on how to put the thing together'!).

Psalm 36:9 says that it is with God that there is the fountain of life; it is in His light that we see light; and the promise set down in the Proverbs of Solomon says that it is when we do not lean on our own understanding but trust in the Lord with all our hearts that he will make our paths straight (Proverbs 3:5–6). When we neglect or rebel against the revelation God has given us, we build on sand and our house will not stand (Matthew 7:26–27).

The need to heed God's own self-revelation can be illustrated from the experience of the woman, mentioned previously who met a well-known actor but could not remember his name. Even when the actor revealed his name, she would not accept it. It is an amusing incident but if that scenario is somewhat bizarre, how much more absurd would it be to say of the revelation *God* has given of Himself, 'No, no, I'll work it out myself'!

God has spoken. 'Under the sun' is not the whole of reality. And Ecclesiastes 3:11 tells of two particular ways in which God has given us His own self-revelation: 'He has made everything beautiful in its time. Also, he has put eternity into man's heart.'

## Everything is beautiful

He has revealed Himself in the beauties of creation. When we look at the beauties of the world around us, we are seeing something of the glory of the God who is the Creator of it all. This is one answer to the doubt about whether life has meaning: as the title of the hymn has it, 'Jesus is Lord! Creation's voice proclaims it,'[11] or in the majestic if somewhat dated language of the poet (based on Psalm 19):

> The spacious firmament on high,
> With all the blue ethereal sky,
> And spangled heavens, a shining frame,
> Their great Original proclaim.
> In reason's ear they all rejoice
> And utter forth a glorious voice,
> For ever singing, as they shine,
> 'The hand that made us is divine'.[12]

Paul wrote in 1 Timothy 6:17, 'As for the rich in this present age, charge them not to be haughty, nor to set their hopes on the uncertainty of riches, but on God, who richly provides us with everything to enjoy.' The faith of the Bible is not a world-denying religion, as has sometimes been implied in notions of having to choose between going God's way or 'enjoying yourself'—as if these are mutually exclusive options. God means people to appreciate and enjoy the glories of this life and of this world—none more so than those who trust in the Creator of it all. All of this world is God's gift to us, for our enjoyment. Christian commitment certainly involves the call for self-denial and sometimes self-sacrifice, but at the same time Jesus spoke of the 'abundant life' He gives to His people (John 10:10). And Ecclesiastes refers to a way of enjoying life as the gift of God. Never mind all those who think that it is in forgetting about God and His ways that true happiness lies—that they are the ones who are having a good time.

The point is made in Ecclesiastes 5:18–19: 'Behold, what I have seen to be good and fitting is to eat and drink and find enjoyment in all the toil with which one toils under the sun the few days of his life that God has given him, for this is his lot. Everyone also to whom God has given wealth and possessions and power to enjoy them, and to accept his lot and rejoice in his toil—this is the gift of God.'

**Eternity in our hearts**

Secondly, Ecclesiastes 3:11 refers to God setting eternity in the hearts of human beings. He has made us in such a way that the things of this world—wonderful as they are when received as gifts from the hand of a loving God—will never satisfy us. They will not bring us that fulfilment, which is God's plan for His creation, that intimacy of relationship with our Maker that has been spoiled by human sin.

For there is the problem. It is not only a matter of whether life has meaning; there is also the question of what is to be done about the sin that has spoiled God's good creation.

And the Bible's answer is that God Himself has done what is necessary. The God who speaks through creation and through the eternity that He has placed in the human heart, has also revealed

Himself in the person and work of Jesus Christ. He is 'the image of the invisible God ... He is before all things, and in him all things hold together' (Colossians 1:15–17).

He came as a human being to redeem us, to restore us to what we were made to be. Because He is divine, He can *save* us and, because He is human, He can save *us*. This is good news, and the call of the gospel is to humble ourselves before Him and receive His forgiveness and salvation. He will then begin the process of making us more Christ-like through the working of His Holy Spirit within.

This is what we learn from God's own self-revelation in the living Word, Jesus Christ, and the written Word, the Bible, which is able to make us wise for salvation through faith in Jesus Christ (2 Timothy 3:15).

Ecclesiastes raises fundamental questions about the meaning of our existence. It argues that if we leave God out of the equation—or rather, out of our lives—then we are condemned to meaninglessness (vanity); we would be driven to the grim conclusion of the novelist, Ernest Hemingway, who won the Pulitzer Prize in 1953 and the Nobel Prize for Literature in 1954 but who shot himself dead in 1961; his conclusion about life was, 'Life is just a dirty trick, a short journey from nothingness to nothingness.'[13]

However, at the end of Ecclesiastes, Solomon wrote, 'The words of the wise are like goads, and like nails firmly fixed are the collected sayings; they are given by one Shepherd' (Ecclesiastes 12:11). Among the sixty-six books of the Bible, perhaps none is more of a goad than Ecclesiastes, with these probing questions about the purpose and meaning of life. It presses home these questions and even doubts in order to point us to faith in the living Lord. Its solemn and dark message is meant to give an answer to doubt and enable us to concur with the hymn-writer in saying:

> We will never doubt Thee,
> Though Thou veil Thy light;
> Life is dark without Thee;
> Death with Thee is bright.
> Light of light, shine o'er us
> On our pilgrim way;
> Go Thou still before us,
> To the endless day.[14]

**NOTES**

1 Martinez P. and Sims A., *Mad or God*, (London, IVP, 2018), p. 150.

2 Postman, Neil, *Amusing Ourselves to Death*, (New York: Penguin, 1985).

3 Quoted in: Chapman, Colin, *Christianity On Trial*, (Berkhamsted: Lion, 1971), p. 48.

4 Hymn by Lawrence Tuttiett, 1825–97.

5 Aitken, Jonathan, *Pride and Perjury*, (London: Harper Collins, 2000), p. 11.

6 Ibid., pp. 8–9.

7 Quoted in *Friday Night Theology* from Evangelical Alliance, 18th May 2012 by Ann Holt of the Bible Society

8 Bakewell, Joan, [ed.], *Belief*, (London: Duckworth, 2005), p. 227.

9 Quoted in: D'Souza, Dinesh, *What's So Great About Christianity?* (Washington, DC: Regnery Publishing, 2007), p. 267.

10 Aitken, Jonathan, *Pride and Perjury*, pp. 361–362.

11 Hymn by David Mansell, (Authentic Publishing, 1982).

12 Joseph Addison, 1672–1719.

13 Quoted in an article in the *Evangelical Times*, Issue 106,6 (March 1995).

14 Hymn, 'Summer suns are glowing' by William Walsham How, 1823–97.

# 6 'How long, O LORD ...?'

## DOUBTS ABOUT THE FAIRNESS OF LIFE

In the last chapter, we considered doubts about the meaning of life. Another significant cause of doubt is the apparent unfairness of life.

Many of us were brought up to think that goodness should be rewarded and wickedness punished, but often it seems as if the opposite is true, and many people have come to the conclusion that it really does not pay to seek always to do the right thing. 'Was it for nothing that I ... kept myself from doing wrong?' is a question asked by many people in many ages. The words actually come from the Psalmist Asaph whom we met earlier.

He speaks for many, generation after generation, in saying that doubt almost brought him to the edge of the cliff; this is part of the New Living Translation of some of its verses:

> I envied the proud when I saw them prosper despite their wickedness. They seem to live such a painless life; their bodies are so healthy and strong. They aren't troubled like other people or plagued with problems like everyone else. These fat cats have everything their hearts could ever wish for! (Psalm 73:3–7).[1]

And so, it goes on: 'people are dismayed and confused, drinking in all their words. "Does God realise what is going on?" they ask' (Psalm 73:2-11 NLT).

Another place where we find the Bible facing up to this source of doubt is the book of the prophet Habakkuk. He gave frank expression to his doubts—or at least questions—about faith. He was bold enough to ask questions about God and His ordering of things, His providence, His apparently strange ways—bold enough indeed to put these questions to God Himself.

One of the commendations of *The God Delusion*[2], which was quoted earlier, says, 'This is my favourite book of all time. I hope that those secure and intelligent enough to see the value of examining their beliefs will be big and strong enough to read this book.' If that implies that we who believe are timid souls who are afraid of anything that might disturb our simple and unquestioning faith, well that certainly does not include Habakkuk. And it need not include any of us.

Most of the prophets were people who addressed people on behalf of God—but Habakkuk questioned God on behalf of the community. He lived during the twilight days of Judah's history before the Babylonian exile. After the battle of Carchemish in 605 BC, Babylon became the world's super-power, and that empire stood behind much of the Old Testament story, as various prophets foresaw judgement coming on Judah's sin and rebellion at the hands of the Babylonians.

This is the situation behind the book of Habakkuk, and behind the words of what is one of the book's best-known phrases, the question of 1:13: 'You who are of purer eyes than to see evil and cannot look at wrong, why do you idly look at traitors and remain silent when the wicked swallows up the man more righteous then he?' How could it be possible that God could use the ruthless and idolatrous Babylonians in His holy purposes?

The book contains very real questions *and* strong faith, and in between we find the revelation God gave him.

## Real questions

Without any introduction, Habakkuk comes straight to the point: 'O Lᴏʀᴅ, how long shall I cry for help, and you will not hear?' (1:2). This the heartfelt cry that bursts out at the very beginning. And if anyone should ask, in terms of logic, why he would put his question *to* God when he says that God does not listen, well that would simply show up the inadequacy of human logic. Even if he feels as if God has closed His ears, it is *to God* that he addresses his complaint and doubt. His is not an easy 'God's in His heaven—all's right with the world!'[3] faith; the problem is precisely that everything seems to be wrong with the world.

In asking how God could possibly use Babylon as His instrument of judgement, he gives expression to a common sentiment. People sometimes say, 'How can you believe in a divine being when there's so much evil in the world, whether you think of the atrocities that are perpetrated on human beings by people who often seem to get away with it, or of tornadoes and tsunamis that ruin lives, disasters, floods, war, violence, and so on.' It is a real question: *'Can we still believe in God in a world of so much evil?'*

The shape of the questions in Habakkuk 1 has a rather contemporary sound as the prophet identifies four things in his questioning of God: violence, conflict, lawlessness and injustice:

- Violence. The second verse of the book asks, 'How long shall I ... cry to you "Violence!" and you will not save?' Why does God not act? Habakkuk says, 'Destruction and violence are before me' (1:3). These are questions which many people would ask today: 'why doesn't God do something about the terrible levels of violence in our world?' People's lives are blighted by strife—mortars, rifles, bombs, terrorist attacks. We should point out that such violence is the result of the actions of human beings, not God; it is human beings who have invented bows and arrows, whips and thumbscrews, racks and crosses, machine guns and nuclear weapons. But even so, the question persists—'why doesn't God do something to punish and/or bring about the end of the world's violence?'

- Conflict. The last words of verse 3 still stand: 'Strife and contention arise.' We hear of ethnic conflict, inter-tribal conflict, international terrorism, gang warfare, and so on.

- Lawlessness. Verse 4 says, 'The law is paralysed.' How often do people say that there does not seem to be the respect for law and order that there once was. We know that the law is unable to deal with the fundamental issue, which is in the fallen hearts of human beings, but we would still like to see more respect for common law and order.

- Injustice. 'Justice never goes forth', he says, and worse, 'The wicked surround the righteous; so justice goes forth perverted' (1:4). We hear complaints about the law courts sometimes appearing to be more concerned to protect criminals than to defend the victims of crime; we hear about people escaping justice on the grounds of technicalities; we hear of punishments and sentences that seem too lenient for terrible crimes. Sometimes it seems that the criminals prosper and the innocent are put under pressure. And in another sense, how many people in today's world would feel that weight of injustice; an aid agency once talked of a country where half of the cultivable land was being used for export crops while more than half of the children born there died of malnutrition before the age of five.

In these ways, we see that the issues which led to Habakkuk's questions and doubts are very like the issues of our day. We can feel the force of the prophet's 'How long shall I cry for help, and you will not hear?'

The other main issue for Habakkuk concerns God's action in response to such questions. God's answer is given in verse 5: 'I am doing a work in your days that you would not believe if told,' and then His next words raised as many questions about God in Habakkuk's mind as His earlier seeming inaction. God was going to raise up the Chaldeans (aka Babylonians), a people who 'march through the breadth of the earth, to seize dwellings not their own' (v. 6). And there follows a vivid description of this 'dreaded and fearsome' nation (v. 7).

God was saying *He* would raise them up! They were going to be the instruments of *His* judgement on Judah's moral and spiritual decline.

How could God do such a thing? This is part of the complaint that Habakkuk brings to God. Everyone knew that Babylon was a powerful and ruthless empire that had no time for the religion of little Judah, and was it not the faith of Israel that God is holy and pure? The prophet protests in verse 12, 'Are you not from everlasting,

O LORD my God, my Holy One?' And in verse 13 he challenges God: are You not of purer eyes than to see evil and look at wrong?

These words have often been interpreted in relation to our personal and individual sins, and to the wonder that God should accept sinners who come to Him just as they are. But in their original setting, the words are a protest against the idea of God working through the ruthless godlessness of the Babylonians. He asks how God, if He is pure and holy, can 'idly look at traitors and remain silent when the wicked swallows up the man more righteous than he' (v. 13).

Yet this was God's plan, and the Bible's message is that God is sovereign and He works out His purposes in many ways and through different events, even when that seems to baffle human understanding.

Western society is not like ancient Israel, but it could be that, as our society sinks further and further into moral decadence, there could come a time when God may act in judgement. We see the rise of various powers in our contemporary world, even nations and groups that are anti-Christian, and there may come a time when we are left asking Habakkuk's question: *Lord, how could you allow anti-Christian powers to over-run our society?* Other systems, religious or non-religious, seem to grow, whether by force in acts of violence and terrorism or through gradual infiltration, while the West, which has been blessed in terms of Christian influence and teaching for a long time, seems bent on throwing away that heritage.

But the Bible insists that God is not mocked. Sooner or later His judgement will fall on wickedness and godlessness. May our western society realize that it has been barking up the wrong tree in our departure from the faith of our fathers and that we need to return to the Lord God in repentance and renewal. Otherwise—if our people maintain this attitude of resolutely turning their backs on God—He may indeed have His ways of dealing with us.

## God's answer

The beginning of Habakkuk, chapter 2, tells of the prophet doing what believers should do in times of confusion or puzzlement—look for God's perspective. 'I will take my stand at my watchpost and station myself on the tower, and look out to see what he will say to me' (v. 1).

A watchtower was obviously the best vantage point from which to see the surrounding countryside. Especially when under attack, a sentry could, from such a position, see the enemy's approach and give warning, because he could see things from there which he could not see at ground level.

And that which would be true in the literal sense was also true spiritually for Habakkuk. To view everything from God's watchtower means gaining a perspective that enables us to see things that we cannot see from a purely worldly angle.

It was when the prophet went up to God's watchtower that 'the LORD answered me' (2:2) and called for Habakkuk's patience and trust.

He called for patience—'The vision awaits its appointed time ... if it seems slow, wait for it; it will surely come' (v. 3). As a famous hymn puts it, 'Here let me wait with patience.'[4] God does not work to our timetable and there are times when His call is to wait patiently on Him. Even if He does not seem to answer all of our questions right now—wait patiently for Him.

And patience goes with trust—the faith that God knows what He is doing, and that (in the words of Genesis 18:25) the Judge of all the earth will do right. God would work out His purposes through the Babylonians even with all their ruthless and godless power.

That certainly did not mean that God approved of their actions or motives, but He can work out His purposes through all manner of means. After all—to refer to the very centre of the Bible's message— God would work out His eternal purpose of salvation through a blood-stained cross on a hill outside Jerusalem.

Who could ever have dreamt it? A cross was an instrument of barbaric torture to a slow and agonizing death; it was a thing of terror and horror, from which anyone would shrink. The Roman lawyer and politician Cicero, for example, said that 'the very word "cross" should be far removed not only from the person of a Roman citizen, but from his thoughts, his eyes and his ears.'[5] Could God work some purpose of good from such a thing?

Yet, Christianity centres in that message of the cross which the apostle Paul said might be a stumbling block to Jews and folly to Gentiles but it is the power and wisdom of God for all who believe in Christ (1 Corinthians 1:23–24), who 'suffered once for sins, the righteous for the unrighteous, that he might bring us to God' (1 Peter 3:18).

In Habakkuk chapter 2, we find the Lord's reply to the prophet's questions. It is not really an answer that explains everything about God's ways (He does not actually owe us an explanation), but it is one that calls for patience and trust, before going on to one of the best-known and most-quoted verses in Habakkuk.

It begins, 'Behold, his soul [Babylon's] is puffed up; it is not upright within him' (v. 4). Even if Babylon should be the instrument of God's judgement upon Judah, that does not mean Babylon was consciously acting as God's agent; so far as they were concerned, it was all about imperial expansion, and the rest of chapter 2 goes on to say that God would ultimately deal with Babylon.

There is a series of five woes—reminders that everyone will have to answer to God sooner or later—and the chapter culminates in another of Habakkuk's famous phrases: 'The LORD is in his holy temple; let all the earth keep silence before him' (v. 20).

But the latter part of verse 4 says, 'But the righteous shall live by his faith.' And, if Romans 1:16–17 forms the 'text' for Romans as a whole, it is significant that Paul there quotes this text from Habakkuk: 'I am not ashamed of the gospel, for it is the power of God for salvation to everyone who believes, to the Jew first and also to the Greek. For in it the righteousness of God is revealed from faith for faith, as it is written, "The righteous shall live by faith".' It is not by achievement or working hard to please God but by faith that people are put right with God. This faith is simply the empty hands which accept all that God gives and believers are then called to work out that salvation (Philippians 2:12) in lives of gratitude and discipleship.

## Renewed faith

It has been suggested that Habakkuk stands among the prophets as Thomas stands among the disciples. And just as Thomas ('doubting Thomas', as he is sometimes called) gave us one of the fullest expressions of faith to be found in Scripture—'My Lord and my God' (John 20:28)—so Habakkuk, in his final chapter, gives a wonderful expression of trust in this God who is working His purposes out as year succeeds to year.

It is a prayer and it begins with an expression of awe before God and a prayer for God to act in a new way: 'Your work, O LORD, do I fear. In the midst of the years, revive it; in the midst of the years make it known; in wrath remember mercy' (3:2). The chapter goes over some of God's great acts in the past and, at the end of verse 16, we find him saying, 'Yet I will quietly wait for the day of trouble to come upon people who invade us.' Babylon might seem to be victorious but in the long run justice will prevail.

A grim twentieth-century illustration is given by Dale Ralph Davis. Referring to the aftermath of the Nuremberg trials of Nazi war criminals in 1946, he wrote:

> After the executions of Nazi celebrities on 16 October, fourteen bodies, including those of Goering (who had 'cheated' by managing suicide), Ribbentrop, Keitel, Rosenberg, Frank, Streicher, Jodl and Seyss-Inquart, were delivered to a Munich crematorium. That same evening a container holding the amassed ashes was driven through the rain into the Bavarian countryside. After an hour's drive the vehicle stopped and the ashes were poured into a muddy ditch. Five or six years before, these men could dominate and intimidate. That night a drizzle washed them away.[6]

One of the other Nazi criminals managed to commit suicide and a newspaper report said that he thus managed to escape justice. Actually, he did not! 'It is appointed for man to die once, and after that comes judgement' (Hebrews 9:27).

Habakkuk is content to await God's timing and he concludes the book with a remarkable expression of faith combined with patience. He has worked through his doubts and, even if he does not know all the answers to all his questions, he prays:

Though the fig tree should not blossom, nor fruit be on the vines, the produce of the olive fail and the fields yield no food, the flock be cut off from the fold and there be no herd in the stalls, yet I will rejoice in the LORD; I will take joy in the God of my salvation. God, the Lord, is my strength (3:17–19).

This is the result of his seeing things from the watchtower.

Even if such dire things should happen, things which in an agrarian society would spell disaster, he had come to the point of trusting God implicitly and believing that He has His purposes in everything that happens and (in New Testament terms), 'For those who love God all things work together for good' (Romans 8:28).

Job went so far as to say, 'Though he slay me, I will hope in him' (Job 13:15). Even if there is violence and conflict and disrespect for law and injustice, still, the Lord is in His holy temple, and His purpose will be done.

This is the practical answer which Scripture gives to our doubts about the seeming unfairness of life. We may not be able to understand and explain everything, but we are encouraged to maintain faith in a living God who does know everything; who works everything into His ultimate sovereign purpose; and whose will shall be done on earth as it is in heaven.

Peter Marshall was a Scottish minister who became chaplain of the United States Senate and, in one of his prayers he said, 'We pray for the bifocals of faith that see the despair and need of the hour but also see, further on, the patience of our God working out His plan in the world He has made.'[7]

May God give us, too, such bifocals so that, even when doubts threaten our faith, we may share the faith of Habakkuk, as paraphrased by the hymn-writer, William Cowper, who suffered with depression and for whom faith was no easy thing:

> Though vine nor fig-tree neither
> Their wonted fruit should bear,
> Though all the fields should wither,
> Nor flocks nor herds be there,
> Yet God, the same abiding,
> His praise shall tune my voice;
> For, while in Him confiding,
> I cannot but rejoice.[8]

**NOTES**

1 *Touch Point Bible*, (Wheaton, Illinois: Tyndale House, 1996), p. 507.
2 Dawkins, Richard, *The God Delusion*, (London: Black Swan, 2007; first published by Bantam Press in 2006).
3 Last line of the 1841 poem, 'Pippa's Song', by Robert Browning. Rintoul, F. and Skinner J. B., *Poets' Quair*, (Edinburgh & London: Oliver & Boyd, 1950), p. 318.
4 'Safe in the arms of Jesus' by Fanny Crosby, 1820–1915.
5 Quoted in many places, including *The Cross of Christ* by John Stott (London: IVP, 1986), p. 24.
6 Davis, D. R., *The Message of Daniel*, (London: IVP, 2013), p. 107. Davis refers to: Read, Anthony, *The Devil's Disciples: Hitler's Inner Circle*, (W. W. Norton, 2003), pp. 922–3.
7 Marshall, Peter, *Mr Jones, Meet the Master*, (London: Fontana, 1980), p. 101.
8 From the hymn, 'Sometimes a light surprises the Christian while he sings', by William Cowper, 1731–1800. It has been written of Cowper that he was 'subject to melancholy and knew more about the darker side of Christian experience than the brighter.' (Murray, John J., *Behind A Frowning Providence*, [Edinburgh: Banner of Truth, 1990]), Introduction.

# 7 Under cover of darkness

## DOUBTS ABOUT THE RELEVANCE OF RELIGION

A long time ago, I had a friend who was involved in Christian activities. He became a church member by profession of faith, he helped in Sunday School, and sometimes gave the message at hospital ward services. He went off to study abroad and then, one day, I received a letter in which he said that he was about to renounce Christianity and become a Muslim. It was a huge shock; he had seemed to be convinced and committed to Christ.

In his book on Doubt, Os Guinness wrote about that kind of scenario. He wrote about being 'deeply saddened by the large number of people who were once professing Christians, but who now claim to have 'lost their faith'. In my experience, a great number of these are people who lacked nothing in terms of orthodox belief or depth of experience but who have never understood why their faith is true.'[1]

The evangelist, Andy Bannister, has told of giving a talk at Aberdeen University on 'The Evidence for the Resurrection'. Afterwards, a student approached him and asked if he had a moment:

> As we chatted, he explained how he had been raised in a Christian home but had abandoned his faith as a teenager because he had concluded that faith, as Mark Twain quipped, 'is believing things you know ain't so'. He looked at me thoughtfully and then said quietly, 'Your talk today has deeply unsettled me. Nobody ever told me there

were *reasons* to believe that Christianity might be true. I think I may need to rethink some things.[2]

Such experiences lead us to think about what might be called *intellectual doubt*.

The New Testament tells of a man who had many religious, social and probably intellectual advantages—someone who found himself drawn to Jesus and yet was held back by doubts about the rationality of it all.

We meet him in John 3 where there are only a few recorded words from his lips. He approached Jesus with respect: 'We know that you are a teacher come from God, for no one can do these signs that you do unless God is with him' (John 3:2).

His second statement is found a couple of verses later when he put the puzzled question to Jesus: 'How can a man be born when he is old? Can he enter a second time into his mother's womb and be born?' (v. 4). And then, after some further words from Jesus, we hear Nicodemus asking, 'How can these things be?' (v. 9).

After that he fades out of the picture and we are left with Jesus speaking—although the man, Nicodemus, turns up again later in John's Gospel, as we shall see. Nicodemus could not get his mind round the things that Jesus was saying and John chapter 3 leaves matters unresolved.

That is quite common in the Bible. Often incidents are left open-ended, as if to challenge readers about their own response to what has been said, as for example with the famous parable of the so-called prodigal son (we are left wondering whether the elder brother did change his attitude and join the party—see Luke 15:25–32).

John does not tell us how Nicodemus responded, but the two references to him, later in John's Gospel, give us grounds for hoping that he did experience a change of mind and heart.

But, in John 3, he is confused by Jesus' words. His attitude in approaching Jesus might have been: *your message, this Christianity, this gospel—it's all very well for the simple people, the common folk of Galilee—but I have some questions I'd like to put to you; I'm attracted by what I know of you, but I have my doubts too.*

We can, of course, be thankful that the Christian message is not only for highly educated people like Nicodemus. The call is addressed to educated and uneducated people. A great intellectual of his time (1466–1536) said that his patron saint was the penitent thief because he was 'saved with so little theology'![3] You do not need theology (in an academic sense) before you can receive God's salvation. It is one of the delightful felicities of John's Gospel that this third chapter tells of the respectable, moral and educated Nicodemus, while the next chapter tells of the un-named woman of Samaria who was probably a social outcast and whose moral life was a shambles. Yet the gospel message was the same for both; the message of forgiveness and new life was addressed to both.

In a sense, the gospel is a simple message to which the simplest person can respond. Whatever our IQ or intellect, the call is to come to Christ with a humble heart and a sincere faith. We also know that people are not persuaded to become Christians by intellect alone, as if they could be argued into the kingdom of heaven. Thank God for a message that talks about Christ knocking at the door and if anyone hears His voice and opens the door, He will come in to that person's life as a Saviour and Master (Revelation 3:20).

But, in Nicodemus, we come to a prominent person who struggled with some of the things Jesus said. He might have agreed with some words written by C. S. Lewis about 'simple faith'. Lewis wrote:

> It is no good asking for a simple religion. After all, real things aren't simple. They look simple, but they're not. (A table) looks simple: but ask a scientist to tell you what it's really made of—all about the atoms and how the light waves rebound from them and hit my eye and what they do to the optic nerve and what it does to my brain—and of course you will find what we call 'seeing a table' lands you in mysteries and complications which you can hardly get to the end of.[4]

John 3 tells us about Nicodemus' religious background, his reluctant approach and his respectful greeting.

**Religious background**

Nicodemus is introduced as 'a man of the Pharisees, ... a ruler of the Jews' (v. 1). We know the Pharisees from the Gospel accounts as people who made big mistakes in their understanding of what it means to please God. They are portrayed as people who were more interested in external actions than the inner disposition of the heart.

In the outspoken words of Jesus Himself, 'You clean the outside of the cup and the plate, but inside they are full of greed and self-indulgence' (Matthew 23:25). He called them hypocrites, using a word that referred to actors who play a part, pretending to be someone other than who they are. That may be good and acceptable in the context of drama and acting, but it is not good and right in living.

However, we can also note that, for all their faults and even with all their mistaken ways, the Pharisees were people who tried hard to live good lives. They would have been regarded as leading religious figures and Nicodemus was a 'ruler of the Jews'—a member of the ruling court, the Sanhedrin. In fact, Jesus addressed him in John 3:10 as '*the* teacher of Israel' (the definite article is there in the Greek); presumably someone who would have been regarded by many as an expert in religious matters.

But, despite all of this, his 'religion' had apparently not brought him fulfilment or satisfaction or the assurance of God's salvation; this we conclude from the fact that he came to Jesus at all. C. S. Lewis drew one of his illustrations from a children's game: 'There comes a moment when the children who have been playing burglars hush suddenly: was that a *real* footstep in the hall? There comes a moment when people who have been dabbling in religion (man's search for God) suddenly draw back. Supposing we really found Him? We never meant it to come to that. Worse still, supposing He had found us.'[5]

Was there something like that in Nicodemus' case? Having had everything more-or-less neatly tied up, so that if you just obeyed the rules, God would be pleased with you—they then heard all this talk about the Man from Nazareth and the new teaching He was bringing; *could it be that we've only been playing at religion up till now and in Him we hear a REAL footstep in the hall?*

For other doubters mentioned in this book, doubt was attempting to draw them *from* faith in the living God; for Nicodemus, doubt was threatening to pull him *towards* faith in this Son of God who was speaking to him. He was entertaining doubts about the negative reaction of his colleagues—was there something *in* this Jesus about whom so many of the common folk were talking?

'Religion', as a human device to placate God, is futile and does not bring satisfaction or fulfilment. You can be highly religious like Nicodemus and yet not be a true Christian at all.

## Reluctant approach

Presumably it was because Nicodemus was 'somebody' in Jewish society that he came to seek out Jesus in the evening, under cover of darkness. He would not want people to know that he was in any way interested in Jesus.

Later, when he came forward to arrange the reverent burial of Jesus' body, he is described specifically as the man 'who earlier had come to Jesus by night' (John 19:39). The description stuck. Jesus, he might have thought, *is not popular with many of my colleagues, and it would not be good for my reputation for orthodoxy to be known to be fraternizing with Him.*

He must have heard reports about Jesus. It was not only the impact His teaching was having with many ordinary people, but Nicodemus referred specifically to the 'signs' that he was performing. The previous chapter had recorded the miracle at Cana in Galilee when Jesus changed water to wine (John 2:1–11) and John added, 'This, the first of his signs, Jesus did at Cana in Galilee, and manifested his glory. And his disciples believed in him' (v. 11). If that was not bad enough from the point of view of the Jewish religious authorities, John 2:23 says, 'When he was in Jerusalem at the Passover Feast, many believed in his name when they saw the signs that he was doing.'

Such things must have come to the ears of Nicodemus and he evidently wanted to investigate for himself. What was going on? Could Jesus possibly be the promised Messiah? There were many questions buzzing around in his head and much that he simply could not put together.

There is a later time when John referred to widespread disbelief among the Jews, but he also reported, 'Nevertheless, many even of the authorities believed in him, but for fear of the Pharisees they did not confess it, so that they would not be put out of the synagogue; for they loved the glory that comes from man more than the glory that comes from God' (John 12:42–43).

Was Nicodemus being pulled in that direction? Would such a fear of others' opinion lead him to doubt all that he was coming to suspect in his heart and soul? Maybe peer pressure does not only affect young people.[6]

In modern culture, in which it is becoming more and more politically incorrect to identify with Jesus and His church; there may be people who prefer to be secret disciples, being reluctant to come out into the open about it and take a stand within their particular set of people. It may be that no one would actually attack you physically for your faith, yet there is still the temptation sometimes to keep quiet.

In Nicodemus' case, there's also John 7:50–51. The religious leaders were debating what to do, and 'Nicodemus, who had gone to him before, and who was one of them, said to them, "Does our law judge a man without first giving him a hearing and learning what he does?"' That obviously stops short of 'Stand up, stand up for Jesus', but at least he spoke up for fairness and justice.

However, Christ's call is for people who are willing to come out into the open. Secret discipleship is not on His agenda; in fact, there is a saying about the hopelessness of secret discipleship—either the secrecy will kill the discipleship or the discipleship will kill the secrecy.

## Respectful greeting

Nicodemus clearly was drawn to Jesus. We learn that from (a) the way in which he addressed Jesus as 'Rabbi', (b) his assertion, 'You are a teacher come from God' and (c) his recognition that Jesus had performed some miracles ('signs') which must have been divinely inspired. Nicodemus did not, in the way of later liberalism, try to explain away this or that element of the miraculous (the boy's generosity with his picnic lunch in John 6:9, for example, simply shaming others to produce the supplies which they had been selfishly keeping to themselves!). Nicodemus was prepared to accept that Jesus has displayed miraculous powers.

And he wanted to question the Man himself, to find out what was going on, to investigate and consider whether there could be any truth in what was being said about Jesus.

Two phrases in particular are recorded. One is his perhaps brusque response to Jesus' words about the necessity of being born again: 'How can a man be born when he is old? Can he enter a second time into his mother's womb and be born?' The other is the plain bafflement revealed in the last words we hear from him in John 3: "How can these things be?" (v. 9).

After that expression of puzzlement and perhaps exasperation, we are left with Jesus words, including that most-quoted word of John

3:16, 'For God so loved the world, that he gave his only Son, that whoever believes in him should not perish but have eternal life.'

Perhaps John is very deliberate in fading out the voice of Nicodemus so that we only hear the authoritative and gracious voice of Christ Himself—the doubts and questions fading into the background as Jesus stands forth more and more as the true Saviour of all who put their trust in Him.

We described Nicodemus as one in whom doubt was pulling him *towards* faith in Jesus, but we are left uncertain at the end of this meeting about whether he did become a disciple. He certainly did the right thing in coming to Jesus in the first place and, although it is not open to us to come in the same way as Nicodemus did, we can come to Him—in the Scriptures that testify to Him (John 5:39), in prayer and within the fellowship of His people.

Luke's Gospel tells of the resurrection of Jesus and how the women told the disciples, 'but these words seemed to them an idle tale, and they did not believe them" (Luke 24:11). That was the initial reaction, but Luke's account goes on: 'But Peter rose and ran to the tomb.' He would go and investigate for himself.

It is this spirit of honest enquiry and investigation that is welcomed by the Lord. It is good that we can gain much through the help and encouragement of other people—and many of us have cause to be thankful for the way in which other people shared the gospel message with us—but there comes a time when you have to find out for yourself and make up your own mind where you stand.

Many years ago, a member of my congregation passed on a little rhyme that refers to the metaphor of the Christian life as a battle to be fought. I do not know the source of it, but it says:

In the world's broad field of battle,
In the bivouac of life,
You will find the Christian soldier
Represented by his wife.

However, no-one can be represented in this matter by anyone else.

And God, we can say reverently, welcomes any amount of enquiry; does not His Word say, 'You will seek me and find me, when you seek me with all your heart' (Jeremiah 29:13)? And did not Jesus say, 'Seek, and you will find; knock, and it will be opened to you' (Matthew 7:7)?

As John 3 goes on, we see Nicodemus fading into the background and we hear the words of Jesus Himself—words like, 'God did not send his Son into the world to condemn the world, but in order that the world might be saved through him' (John 3:17). That is good news.

And the next verse presses the issue of the response we need to make: 'Whoever believes in him is not condemned, but whoever does not believe is condemned already, because he has not believed in the name of the only Son of God. And this is the judgement: the light has come into the world, and people loved the darkness rather than the light' (John 3:18–19).

We have been thinking of Nicodemus' response to Jesus; but it is more important to consider Jesus' response to Nicodemus. We have referred to Nicodemus' respectful greeting—or was there a note of condescension in it? Whatever is true about that, Jesus cut straight to the heart of everything. It is no doubt a summarized version of the conversation (perhaps recounted later by Nicodemus himself—there were presumably only the two people present) and we do not know whether there were other things said between verses 2 and 3, but there is Jesus' word: 'Truly, truly, I say to you, unless one is born again, he cannot see the kingdom of God.' That cuts through any flattery there may have been; it comes straight to the point.

Jesus did not say, 'Unless you are very religious, you will never enter the kingdom'; He did not say, 'Unless you try your hardest to live a good life, you will never see the kingdom of heaven'; He did not say, 'Unless you go to church regularly, you will never enter the kingdom.' Rather, He said, 'Unless one is born of water and the Spirit, he cannot enter the kingdom of God' (v. 5).

'Water' may refer to our natural birth or to water baptism, but the indispensable necessity is being born of the Spirit. It is a text which brings us right up against the mystery of divine providence because that very image—being born—is passive. In our natural birth, none of us asked to be born or had anything to do with it. And in the realm of the Spirit, this is not fundamentally something we do. As the hymn says:

> My Lord, I did not choose you,
> for that could never be;
> this heart would still refuse you,
> had you not chosen me.[7]

It goes on:

> Unless your grace had called me
> and taught my opening mind,
> the world would have enthralled me,
> to heavenly glories blind:
> my heart knows none above you,

for You I long, I thirst;

and know that if I love you,

Lord, you have loved me first.

Yet we *are* called to respond to His call. He has given us free will, and the gospel call is to repent of our sin and put our faith in Him as our Saviour for this life and for eternity.

The phrase, 'born again', has had a bad press, perhaps because of its casual use by some who think Christianity is simply about putting up your hand at a meeting and then going on as before with a bland confidence that you are on your way to heaven.

But the other place where the expression is used emphasizes that being born again is the beginning of a new life. 1 Peter 1:22–23: 'Love one another earnestly from a pure heart, since you have been born again, not of perishable seed but of imperishable, through the living and abiding word of God.' And a few verses later Peter went on: 'So put away all malice and all deceit and hypocrisy and envy and all slander. Like newborn infants, long for the pure spiritual milk, that by it you may grow up into salvation' (1 Peter 2:1–2).

This is the result and the outworking of being born again and, although that expression is not very common in the Bible, the theme is presented consistently—that Christianity is about a new life. Sometimes in the natural realm people say things like, 'Babies aren't babies long enough,' but we *do* want them to grow up, and similarly, in the spiritual realm, birth is to be followed by growth.

## Nicodemus later

John 3:9 leaves us with Nicodemus saying, 'How can these things be?' But he features on two other occasions later in John's Gospel.

On the first occasion, which we have mentioned already, he was prepared to speak up for fairness and justice—*a person should not be condemned without a fair hearing*. And on the other occasion, we find him coming into the open by tending Jesus' body after the crucifixion. Some might say, 'A bit late in the day'—but of course it was not really late in the day at all; it was the beginning of a wonderful new day.

Had he overcome doubt to become a believer? Had his doubts about the general Jewish rejection of Jesus led him to become a Christian?

There is not any record of him speaking up in the Sanhedrin at the time of Jesus' trial. It could be that he absented himself so as to avoid being put on the spot or could it even be that he was not informed of the hastily called meeting of the Sanhedrin (the others may have been suspicious about where his real loyalties lay)? Perhaps John 19:39–40 does indicate that he had 'come out' as a believer: along with Joseph of Arimathea, 'Nicodemus also, who earlier had come to Jesus by night, came bringing a mixture of myrrh and aloes, about seventy-five pounds in weight. So they took the body of Jesus and bound it in linen cloths with the spices' and then laid it in the garden tomb.

We may entertain the hope that, for Nicodemus, doubt of his previous beliefs and of the attitude being taken by so many towards Jesus had led him through to committed faith. It must have taken considerable courage to come out into the open, even though people at that stage had no idea of the truly sensational event that was about to happen when Jesus would come crashing through the gates of death from the other side.

It might be said that if Nicodemus had become a true and open believer, we would have expected to hear something more of him later in the story (perhaps in the book of Acts). Possibly that it true, and there can be no certainty about his final response to Christ, the One who said to Nicodemus that God so loved the world that whoever—religious leader or someone with no previous knowledge of Jesus at all, upright sinner like Nicodemus or downright sinner, educated or uneducated—anyone who believes in Him should not perish but have everlasting life. We may indeed hope that doubt of his previous rejection of Jesus led him to real and committed faith.

**NOTES**

1 Guinness, Os, *Doubt*, p. 85.

2 https://stpeters-dundee.org.uk/2017/12/12/christianity-in-scotland/ (accessed 14/09/23).

3 Attributed to Desiderius Erasmus in: Bainton, Roland, *Here I stand: A Life of Martin Luther*, (Nashville: Abingdon Press, 1950 edition), p. 98.

4 https://wondrouscross.wordpress.com/category/cs-lewis/ (accessed 14/09/23)

5 Lewis, C. S., *Miracles*, (London & Glasgow: Collins, 1947), p. 98.

6 An interesting allusion to Nicodemus' story is found in the account of the eighteenth-century evangelical movement, during which the Countess of Huntingdon had a church building erected in the city of Bath. 'In later months an unusual feature was added. Lady Betty Cobbe, daughter-in-law of the Archbishop of Dublin, after her own conversion, was active in influencing Bishops and other members of the clergy, during their visits to Bath, to attend these evangelical services. In order that they might hear without the disgrace of being seen, one or two seats immediately inside the door were heavily curtained off, and Lady Betty facetiously dubbed the area 'The Nicodemus Corner.'' Dallimore, Arnold, *George Whitefield*, (Edinburgh: Banner of Truth, 1980), p. 458.

7 Hymn by Josiah Conder, 1789–1855. *Praise! Book*, (Darlington: Praise Trust, 2000), No. 691.

# 8 'Are you the one?'

## DOUBTS ABOUT THE METHODS OF JESUS

The fact that a person has been an upfront follower of Jesus—someone who has publicly nailed his or her colours to the mast—does not mean that that person is immune to doubts. Doubt can creep up even on people who have been believers for a long time and who have been active in the Lord's service. Things happen—or do not happen—that lead them to wonder whether it has all been a mistake. Have we made too-big claims for Christianity, or even for Christ? We would not stop believing but do we need to modify (i.e., tone down) our beliefs.

It happened with such a forthright disciple—the man known as John the Baptist. There was no doubting his faith credentials; he was the man who prepared the way for Christ, who pointed Him out as the Lamb of God who takes away the sin of the world (John 1:29) and who stood up strongly for high standards of morality.

Yet, at one point in his life we find him expressing serious doubts about Jesus.

In many ways John can be seen as a bridge from the Old Testament to the New Testament, and many people would think that, once we cross that bridge, doubt would be a thing of the past. Does the New Testament not tell of the fulfilment of the prophecies of old: does it not describe Jesus as the suffering servant of the Lord who would bear the sin of many (Isaiah 53) and is the New Testament not full of the note of conviction and undoubting faith?

- 'Faith is the assurance of things hoped for, the conviction of things not seen' (Hebrews 11:1).
- 'I know whom I have believed, and I am convinced that he is able to guard until that day what has been entrusted to me' (2 Timothy 1:12).
- '... we have confidence before God' (1 John 3:21).
- 'We know that for those who love God all things work together for good' (Romans 8:28).
- 'I am sure that neither death nor life ... nor anything else in all creation, will be able to separate us from the love of God in Christ Jesus our Lord' (Romans 8:38–9).

Such phrases are striking—'we know', 'I am convinced', 'we have confidence', 'I am sure'—but, although that note of conviction and assurance is indeed the dominant theme of the New Testament, we also find instances of doubt there.

And in the case of John the Baptist, Luke 7:19 tells of a message he sent to Jesus: 'Are you the one who is to come, or shall we look for another?'

John was confined in a prison cell and we find him wondering about all that was happening: had he been right to identify Jesus as the expected Messiah, or had he been misled and carried away on a tide of emotion? As we think about John's perplexity, we may consider the background, the question and the answer.

## The background

One certain thing about John is that he was no faint-hearted or half-hearted follower of Jesus. Jesus Himself said John was not like a reed shaken by the wind (Luke 7:24), as if he would blow this way at one moment and another way at another moment. In the time of the American civil war there was a house near the border between north and south where the owners kept two flags. When the union army was passing by, they flew the union flag and when the army of the southern confederate states passed, they flew the confederate flag. John would have had no truck with such a practice (later, incidentally, that house came under attack from both sides).

Mark started his Gospel account with John: 'The beginning of the gospel of Jesus Christ, the Son of God. As it is written in Isaiah the prophet, "Behold, I send my messenger before your face, who will prepare your way, the voice of one crying in the wilderness: 'Prepare the way of the Lord, make his paths straight.'"' (Mark 1:1–3). He went on immediately to tell of John's appearance in the wilderness as a strange man clothed in camel's hair and eating locusts and wild honey, proclaiming, 'After me comes he who is mightier than I, the strap of whose sandals I am not worthy to stoop down and untie' (Mark 1:6–8).

He was a fiery preacher—forthright and perhaps rather fearsome—with his message of God's righteousness and the judgement that lay ahead for the impenitent. He proclaimed a baptism of repentance and, among the many who came out be baptized by him, Jesus came, not to confess His sins, but to identify Himself with the sinners He had come to save.

The writer of the fourth Gospel gives us the words quoted above: 'Behold, the Lamb of God, who takes away the sin of the world!' (John 1:29). Later, when John was told that Jesus was gaining more converts then he, he explained that that was inevitable; it was what was meant to happen. 'He must increase, but I must decrease' (John

3:30). And Jesus Himself said of John, 'Among those born of women none is greater than John' (Luke 7:28).

Yet, despite all of that background, we find John entertaining doubts and wondering: 'Could it be that I've been mistaken? Have I been carried away? Have I made a fool of myself by sticking my neck out so far for Him?'

It is significant that this episode is in the New Testament at all— that it was not suppressed as a bad example or omitted out of later deference to the memory of John. One of the characteristics of the Bible is its honesty; no attempt is made to paper over the cracks. Even its heroes and heroines have 'feet of clay' (Daniel 2:34). Consider the following list:

- Noah got drunk (Genesis 9:21).
- Abraham lied (Genesis 12:13).
- Sarah laughed at God's promises (Genesis 18:12).
- Jacob was a schemer (Genesis 25:29–34).
- Moses killed someone (Exodus 2:12).
- Samson was a womaniser (Judges 16:1).
- David committed adultery and murder (2 Samuel 11).
- Jonah tried to run away from God (Jonah 1:3).
- The disciples fell asleep while Jesus prayed (Matthew 26:40).
- Peter denied that he even knew Jesus (Matthew 26:70).
- Thomas doubted the resurrection (John 20:25).
- Paul (Saul) persecuted Christians (Acts 8:3).
- Euodia and Syntyche fell out with each other (Philippians 4:2).
- Barnabas and Paul had a serious disagreement (Acts 15:39).

God works through imperfect people, clay vessels (2 Corinthians 4:7), and the fact that even such a stalwart as John the Baptist passed through this time of doubt can be an encouragement for others who have problems. Consider two individuals who are imaginary and yet real:

- One is Ian who had given little thought to the message of Christianity until, out of curiosity, he accepted an invitation from a friend to attend a meeting at which a speaker explained the gospel message in such a way that Ian was captivated. Everything seemed to fall into place and he was converted there and then. He came to wonder why he had not discovered this wonderful gospel message much earlier and he also wondered why everybody else did not see it.

  He was convinced, and he was sure that his family and friends would make the same discovery; all he had to do was tell them the good news of Christ and His forgiveness, and other people would fall on their knees too. But then he found that it did not actually happen like that. He saw that other people could not understand why he had 'gone all religious'; they were mystified about what Ian saw in it all. And gradually Ian began to wonder, even to consider whether he had actually been duped or perhaps carried away emotionally.

- The other person is Frances who had been brought up to believe in God, Jesus and the Bible. She had happily accepted all that she was taught and seemed to everyone a model of the stable Christian. She was involved in various kinds of Christian work—taught a Junior Church class and helped with the youth club, even taking her turn at delivering the God-slot.

  Most people would have imagined that she was immune to doubt but, in the inner recesses of Frances' mind, things were different. At work she faced mockery because of her faith; at first it seemed like humorous banter but as time went by it 'got to' her and she found in herself more and more of a desire to just fit in with the crowd around her. Breathing daily the suffocating air of secularism, she sometimes even wondered whether all that she had assumed to be true was maybe a huge con. People asked questions which she could not answer and she found herself tempted to play down her commitment—not really to jettison faith, but to wonder whether Christianity was not so much the truth as an aspect of truth, and Jesus not so much the way as a way to God—one among many. Maybe there was something more to come, another great and wonderful Messiah-figure who would come and bring in a utopian world of perfection.

Yes, John the Baptist's experience may be replicated in different ways; even strong faith may sometimes be troubled by doubt, as with John 'calling two of his disciples to him ... (and sending) them to the Lord, saying, "Are you the one who is to come, or should we look for another?"' (Luke 7:19).

## The question

He was not sure any longer whether he should regard Jesus as the promised Messiah; perhaps He was simply another forerunner of the Messiah.

Reports were reaching John in his lonely prison of some amazing things that were being done by Jesus, but (he wondered) was there something lacking? His question was not necessarily putting Jesus down. He did not doubt that Jesus was special and wonderful, but was it possible that Jesus too, like John, had been sent to prepare the way for a greater one still to come?

Obviously, we see the story after the event; we know the outcome, especially the way in which Jesus would offer His life as a ransom for many—the Lamb of God who would bear away the sin of the world; the One on whom the Lord laid the iniquity of us all.

But, of course, John could not see ahead; he did not know what was going to happen—and the prospects did not look too good! His doubt arose from the totally unfair way in which he was being treated and the wholly unexpected way in which Jesus was acting.

## A) THE UNFAIR WAY HE WAS BEING TREATED

Why was John in prison? It was not for any crime—unless confronting sin is a crime. Luke 3:18–20 tells us that John preached good news to the people: 'But Herod the tetrarch, who had been reproved by him for Herodias, his brother's wife, and for all the evil things that Herod had done, added this to them all, that he locked up John in prison.' Herod wanted to silence John's bothersome voice; he would lock him away where the pesky prophet could not do any more harm.

My Study Bible gives a useful summary of the sordid story: 'Herod Antipas loved Herodias, the wife of his half-brother Herod Philip I. Both were married at the time. Herodias divorced Herod Philip I and Herod Antipas divorced his wife, and they married. John the Baptist had publicly condemned Herod Antipas for his actions.'[1] John did not tailor his message for his audience. Herod or no Herod, if a thing is wrong, it is wrong.

And, of course, Herod did not like being confronted with his wrongdoing. He exercised his dictatorial power and had John arrested and imprisoned.

It was totally unfair and unjust. John might have thought that if God is a righteous God (and it was for insisting on that that he was in prison) and if Jesus really were the promised Messiah of God, then how come he was still suffering this unjust imprisonment? Had God forgotten about him? And why hadn't the Son of God (if that's who Jesus was) taken action on his behalf? The whole reason why he was in prison was that he had been faithful to the ways of God and steadfast in his assertion of God's truth.

That was the question: could Jesus really be the Messiah while he was left in that prison? It is a question that could still be voiced in our very different world. If Jesus really is the Messiah and Saviour which the Bible says He is, then why is there still so much injustice, inequality and iniquity in the world—so many things that pollute God's creation?

The question may be asked at the very personal level: if God is God, if Jesus is the Son of God, why has this or that happened to me? Why haven't my prayers been answered? Why hasn't my relative or friend been healed? And so on.

And it may be asked on the larger scale: if Christianity is true and Jesus is who Christians claim He is, then why isn't the world a much better place than it is?

There is, of course, the fact that we human beings have so often ignored or rebelled against God and His ways. The famous Alexander Solzhenitsyn made the point when he looked back with this recollection:

When I started going to school in Rostov-on-Don—passing on my way a glittering sign of the League of Militant Atheists—schoolchildren taunted me for accompanying my mother to the last remaining church in town and tore the cross from around my neck. Later, I recall hearing a number of older people offer this explanation for the great disasters that had befallen Russia: 'Men have forgotten God; that's why all this has happened.' Since then, I have spent more than fifty years working on the history of the Russian Revolution; in the process I have read hundreds of books, collected hundreds of personal testimonies, and have already contributed eight volumes of my own towards the effort of clearing away the rubble left by the upheaval. But if I were asked today to formulate as concisely as possible the main cause of the ruinous Revolution that swallowed up some sixty million of our people, I could not put it more accurately than to repeat: 'Men have forgotten God; that's why all this has happened'.

It is worth quoting more of this remarkable testimony, since Solzhenitsyn went on to refer to a wider application:

The West has yet to experience a Communist invasion and religion is free. But the West, too, is experiencing a drying up of religious consciousness. This gradual sapping of strength from within is a threat to faith that is perhaps even more dangerous than any attempt to assault religion violently from without. Imperceptibly, through decades of gradual erosion, the meaning of life in the West has ceased to be seen as anything more lofty than the 'pursuit of happiness'. The concepts of good and evil have been ridiculed, banished from common use.... To the ill-considered hopes of the last two centuries we can propose only a determined quest for the warm hand of God, which we have so rashly and self-confidently spurned.[2]

In biblical language, 'The LORD's hand is not shortened, that it cannot save, or his ear dull, that it cannot hear; but your iniquities have made a separation between you and your God, and your sins have hidden his face from you so that he does not hear' (Isaiah 59:1–2).

However, even after such considerations, we still see John troubled by this question: was Jesus really the promised One or should they be looking for someone still to come? Was there even something of the feeling, 'If you are the one who was to come, then get on with it, launch your crusade, make a bigger impact.'

But, besides the unfair way John was being treated, there was:

### B) THE UNEXPECTED WAY JESUS WAS ACTING.

In those days of political oppression under Rome, many Jews would have expected that, when the Messiah came, he would be a freedom-fighter, a fierce warrior who would lead a nationalist movement—a political Messiah. Jesus did not fit that description.

John would not have shared such expectations, but perhaps he did expect something much more dramatic—and speedy—than what could be seen in Jesus. In that sense, there is disappointment in John's question.

What had Jesus done? Had He taken the world by storm? No, He had not. He had gathered a few disciples about Him, although they were not particularly powerful or influential people by any earthly standards. He had seemed to be content to go around teaching people wherever people would listen. As for the people who mattered in the society of that time, He had quickly fallen foul of them, especially the religious leaders whom He might have been expected to court and get on side. There had been miracles, of course, even amazing things like the raising of the widow of Nain's son in the chapter which tells of John's question.

These things were true, but still, the heather had not been set on fire with renewal and passion. And John was left wondering about it all; had he been mistaken after all?

It can happen for our imaginary Ian and Frances also. They came to faith in different ways but for both, everything seemed so wonderful, so new, so exciting. Even their view of the world had changed; they would have agreed with the sentiment of the nineteenth-century hymn that says:

> Heaven above is softer blue,
> Earth around is sweeter green;
> Something lives in every hue
> Christless eyes have never seen;
> Birds with gladder songs o'erflow,
> Flowers with deeper beauties shine,
> Since I know, as now I know,
> I am His and He is mine.[3]

In the euphoria of new discovery, Ian and Frances really thought that the kingdom had come and it was only a matter of time until others would come to see what they had seen. But, as time passed and as progress seemed so slow, the nagging questions insinuated themselves into their minds: Have we been mistaken? Is it all just a fairy-tale, a nice idea that doesn't actually relate to the real world?

Like John, they expected to see something more dramatic, more spectacular and more speedy than they did see. The devil can still use that kind of disappointment and promote impatience.

Even if they were to read Jesus' parable of the seed growing secretly—'The kingdom of God is as if a man should scatter seed on the ground. He sleeps and rises night and day, and the seed sprouts and grows; he knows not how. The earth produces by itself, first the blade, then the ear, then the full grain in the ear' (Mark 4:26–28)— still they wonder why God does not act more unmistakeably, and sooner.

Perhaps, especially today in our western secularized society, there are some who wonder at the seeming inactivity of the Lord, or His allowing the forces of atheistic and materialistic secularism to take over—Why doesn't He just zap our land with spiritual power? Why does He allow people to spit in His face so continuously?

With John, these two things—the unfair way he had been treated and the unexpected way Jesus was acting—led to his doubt and question: 'Are you the one who is to come, or should we look for another?'

Incidentally, as with other Bible doubters, we see John bringing his doubts to Jesus, and we are reminded that is the best thing to do with them—rather than allowing them to drive us away from Him, to bring them all to Him.

### The answer

Luke's account tells us:

> In that hour he [Jesus] healed many people of diseases and plagues and evil spirits, and on many who were blind he bestowed sight. And he answered them, 'Go and tell John what you have seen and heard:

the blind receive their sight, the lame walk, lepers are cleansed, and the deaf hear, the dead are raised up, the poor have good news preached to them. And blessed is the one who is not offended by me' (Luke 7:21–23).

Jesus' answer was to point to the fulfilment of the Scriptures in Himself. A few chapters earlier, Luke had reported on Jesus' sermon in the synagogue at Nazareth (Luke 4:16–21). He 'unrolled the scroll and found the place where it was written, "The Spirit of the Lord is upon me, because he has anointed me to proclaim good news to the poor. He has sent me to proclaim liberty to the captives and recovering of sight to the blind, to set at liberty those who are oppressed, to proclaim the year of the Lord's favour."'

And then, when Jesus 'rolled up the scroll and gave it back to the attendant', we are told that 'the eyes of all in the synagogue were fixed on him,' and we can only imagine them looking at one another in astonishment as they heard this carpenter's son, from their own town, say, 'Today this Scripture has been fulfilled in your hearing.' Was He really claiming to be the fulfilment of the Messianic prophecies in Isaiah 61 of the Lord's Servant who would do these very things that Jesus mentioned?

Now, when John's messengers passed on John's troubled question, Jesus answered in the same vein. He pointed to the fulfilment of Scripture in Himself—the fulfilment *of Scripture*, not any popular ideas of what the Messiah would be like. The things to which he referred were the very things that were prophesied as signs of the Messiah. Jesus was, in effect, saying, 'Yes, I am the One who was to come; you needn't look for any other.'

It is His answer to our doubts too. He is the One prophesied in past ages, the Messiah, the Christ of God, who came to do all these things—and more—for He came to give His life as a ransom for many (Mark 10:45).

Surprisingly perhaps, we are not told of John's reaction. Luke does not tell us what happened after that; we are left to presume that he did come to see that, even if it was not in the way he expected, the kingdom had indeed come in Jesus and that Jesus truly was the Messiah and Saviour. He had not been mistaken; there was no need to abandon his earlier faith, no need to look for anyone else. For, as Paul would later draw out about Jesus:

> He is the image of the invisible God, the firstborn of all creation ...
> And he is before all things, and in him all things hold together. And
> he is the head of the body, the church. He is the beginning, the
> firstborn from the dead, that in everything he might be pre-eminent.
> For in him all the fulness of God was pleased to dwell' (Colossians
> 1:15–19.)

John was not to look for another. Neither are we. It is Jesus who is the promised Messiah, the Saviour. He said, 'Go and tell John what you have seen and heard' (Luke 7:22). We too should consider the things that we have seen and heard through the testimony of 'the sacred writings, which are able to make you wise for salvation through faith in Christ Jesus. All Scripture is breathed out by God and profitable' for us (2 Timothy 3:15–16).

We have the record of these days of His earthly ministry. He was giving sight to the blind, hearing to the deaf, and so on. And there may be times still when such unexplainable and miraculous things happen—people healed when all medical help has failed, people being restored to health.

And in other senses too, even though Jesus is no longer physically present, we see:

- people blind to spiritual truth having their eyes opened to see the reality of the Saviour and the glory of the gospel, so that they sing, 'I once was blind but now I see.'[4]
- people crippled by life and its trials receiving the power of Christ to enable them to walk tall—not in self-congratulation but walking in the light of the Lord.
- people being not only physically healed but made clean by having their sins forgiven.
- people who were deaf to spiritual realities having their ears opened to the sweet sound of the gospel of Christ.
- people, 'dead in trespasses and sins' (Ephesians 2:1), raised to new life in Christ.
- poor people hearing the gospel—whether poor economically or spiritually—as they come to trust in Christ.

As Michael Green wrote about the idea that the resurrection of Jesus was simply a hallucination:

> This message of a risen Lord had a force for good which no hallucination has ever had. Through the risen Christ, families were united after years of estrangement, immoral men became chaste and self-centred men become filled with love for others. Wherever it has gone, this gospel has changed the characters of those who received it, and it still does. Some hallucination![5]

In Jesus' response to John, we hear Him saying, 'Blessed is the one who is not offended by me' (Luke 7:23). That was the message to send back to John—and to us: *whatever your situation, whatever injustices there may be all around you and however mysterious the ways of the Lord may sometimes seem, hold fast, don't fall away, rely on Me and My Word.*

That was followed by Jesus' reference to John as not 'a reed shaken by the wind', blowing this way or that according to whichever way the social wind was blowing—merely going with the flow. Rather, John was one who would stand fast. 'A prophet? Yes, I tell you, and more than a prophet.'

And He added, 'I tell you, among those born of women none is greater than John. Yet the one who is least in the kingdom of God is greater than he' (Luke 7:24–28). The humblest believer—then or now—who knows Jesus as Saviour and King has entered into a greater reality than even John knew.

It is the point Jesus made a few pages further on when He said to His disciples, 'Blessed are the eyes that see what you see! For I tell you that many prophets and kings desired to see what you see, and did not see it, and to hear what you hear, and did not hear it' (Luke 10:23–24).

This is a reminder of our great privilege in knowing the gospel of Jesus Christ; it is something that thousands of people would have loved to know, something which thousands of people still do not know. What a privilege it is to know the message of this good news, to know Him as our Saviour, Redeemer and Lord.

And if we sometimes wonder if it is all true—if everything about Jesus is really true—we can bring even that *to* Jesus, as John did, in order that we may hear His reply and, through it, have our doubts answered and have a stronger faith in the One whom John called 'the Lamb of God, who takes away the sin of the world' (John 1:29).

## NOTES

1 *ESV Student Study Bible* (London: Collins, 2011), p. 1265.

2 'Men Have Forgotten God', *Reader's Digest*, February 1989, pp. 109–111.

3 Hymn, 'Loved with everlasting love', by George Wade Robinson, 1838–77. The experience is illustrated in the testimony of D. L. Moody who said that after he had surrendered his life to Christ in 1854, 'The old sun shone a good deal brighter than it ever had before—I felt that it was just smiling upon me; and as I walked out upon Boston Common and heard the birds singing in the trees, I thought they were all singing a song to me.' http://regenerated.net/examples/moody.html (accessed 14/09/23)

4 From the hymn, 'Amazing Grace', by John Newton (1725–1807).

5 Green, Michael, *Man Alive!* (London: IVP, 1967), pp. 48–49.

# 9 'You of little faith'

## DOUBTS ABOUT THE POWER OF JESUS

The actual word, 'doubt', is not found very often in the Bible. The concordance I use has many columns of references in tiny print to 'faith', 'faithfulness', 'believe', 'believers' and such like, but only part of one column lists references to the words, 'doubt' and 'doubting'.[1] Even some of those are in phrases like, 'No doubt this man is a murderer' (Acts 28:4), and the ironic, 'No doubt you are the people ...' (Job 12:2).

One of the few places where the word *is* used, in the sense we are considering in this book, is Matthew 14:31 where we find it in Jesus' question to someone who would not normally be considered a doubter—Peter.

Peter was one of the first to respond to Jesus' call to discipleship (Mark 1:16–20) and the one who gave voice to the faith that Jesus was the promised Christ or Messiah (Mark 8:29). When Jesus was arrested, Peter followed Him 'right into the courtyard of the high priest' (Mark 14:54), and later, he emerged as effectively the leader of the young church (Acts 1:15). In his writing, he encouraged other believers to be ready to give an 'apology'[2] to anyone who asked for a reason for Christian hope (1 Peter 3:15) and he encouraged Christians under pressure to stand firm in their faith (1 Peter 5:9).

Yet it was to this stalwart that Jesus addressed the question, 'Why did you doubt?' (Matthew 14:31). Peter, of all people, probably the most forthright of all the disciples, faced that question from Christ

Himself. Jesus even addressed him as, 'You of little faith' (one word in Greek—'little-faith'). So, as we've learned already, if we have doubts, at least we're in good company!

The word used for 'doubt' in Jesus' question is found only twice in the New Testament: here and in Matthew 28:17 where the disciples saw the risen Christ 'but some doubted'. The Greek word has the prefix, 'dis', which indicates 'two'. They were in two minds—that is what the word suggests, and that is how doubt has been defined—'Faith in two minds'.[3] It refers to people who are inclined to trust in Jesus, and yet there is also the pull of unbelief. Doubt is caught in the middle—pulled from both ends.

The question, 'Why did you doubt?', is found in the record of an incident where we see both a reflection of Peter's character and the remedy for his doubts (Matthew 14:22–32). It is the record of a miracle, but for us there is a parable in the miracle; it reminds us of the importance of keeping our focus on the Lord Himself rather than allowing ourselves to be deflected from following Him. It is when we take our eyes off Him and look at other things—in terms of the story, the wind and waves, which can stand for the troubled circumstances of our lives—it is then that we get into difficulty and begin to sink; doubt creeps in and we need to cry with Peter, 'Lord, save me' (Matthew 14:30).

### Peter's character

The request of Matthew 14:28—'Lord, if it is you, command me to come to you on the water'—is *so Peter*, as we say. It fits the picture we have of him from the Gospel accounts: Peter, the impetuous one.

Jesus had sent the disciples across the lake by boat, while He sought peace for prayer, and it was in the 'wee small hours' that Jesus came to them, walking on the water. It is the kind of thing that baffles our minds; it is beyond our comprehension. But then, if Jesus really is the Son of God who made the world and everything in it (John 1:3), and if He is the One who would eventually show Himself as Lord over death in the greatest miracle of all, then why should He not, for particular reasons of His own, overcome the very laws of nature which He established?

Matthew's account tells of the disciples' terror at the sight of this figure coming across the water in the darkness; they thought it was a ghost ('*phantasma*' in Greek) and they 'cried out in fear'—until they heard the familiar voice saying, 'Take heart; it is I. Do not be afraid' (v. 27).

It is a wonderful word of assurance. Jesus, in a different but nonetheless real sense, comes across the troubled waters of life's trials and hardships and says the same thing to us: 'Take heart; it is I.' The words are literally, 'I am', which reminds us of the divine name revealed long before to Moses (Exodus 3:14): 'Take heart; I am.' If we have times when we seem to be battling with storms and they threaten to overwhelm us, may God give us the faith to hear that voice that says to us: *don't be afraid; I'm here.*

In Peter's case, out he comes with this impetuous request, 'Lord, if it is you, command me to come to you on the water' (v. 28).

## A remedy for his doubts

Jesus simply said, 'Come', and we are told that Peter got out of boat. But then, verse 30 tells us, in the words of the old joke, that he fell flat on his faith. 'When he saw the wind, he was afraid, and beginning to sink he cried out, 'Lord, save me'.

Here is Peter's doubt as he moved the focus of his attention away from Jesus to the adverse circumstances all around him. So long as he kept his eyes on Jesus, everything was fine, but he began to go down when he lost sight of Jesus and concentrated on the storm.

Peter getting out of the boat is a picture of the Christian life, because it requires faith to really accept the authority and lordship of Christ—to receive what He gives through His life, death and resurrection. As Peter had to actually put his feet over the side of the boat, so we are called to actually put our faith in Jesus, receiving His gift of salvation and entrusting ourselves to Him for this life and for eternity.

And if that is the beginning of the Christian life, then 'looking to Jesus' (Hebrews 12:2) is the continuance of it. In Hebrews, the picture of a race is used: 'Let us run with endurance the race that is set before us, looking to Jesus, the founder and perfecter of our faith' (Hebrews 12:1–2). Christianity certainly involves obedience to the Ten Commandments and the golden rule (Mark 12:30–31); it involves attending church and supporting the church's work. But fundamentally it is an attitude of faith in and commitment to the Lord Jesus, and that attitude of faith is pictured in this story of Peter walking across the troubled waters with his eyes fixed on Jesus.

However, it is Peter's doubt that we are considering. He took his focus off Jesus and began to concentrate on the violence of the storm around him, and it is easy, in another sense, for us to allow the fierceness of various storms to take *our* focus off Jesus, so that we begin to sink.

This is true about the storm beating against the Christian cause today. For a long time, the culture could be said to have been apathetic towards the faith, but now there is an aggressive attitude on the part of many people and institutions. Such attacks may be relatively minor compared with the kind of attacks that are made against Christians and churches in many parts of the world—as documented by Barnabas Aid, Christian Solidarity Worldwide, Steadfast Global and other organizations—but we do see attempts to play down Christian influence on life and even to undermine the basic biblical values that have for centuries been the foundation of our social life.

In contemporary western society, it seems that certain views are not to be tolerated. Out of many examples that could be given, we mention as a sample:

- 'A Christian magistrate has been removed from office by the Lord Chancellor after sharing his conviction in a media interview that there is not enough evidence to show that placing children in the care of same sex couples is in their best interests.' He had been a magistrate for fifteen years and had stated in the interview that 'there is a lack of reliable psychological or educational research concerning the effects on children, as in the UK not enough of the children placed in same sex households over the past ten years have yet reached an age beyond puberty.'[4]
- 'A Christian student was removed from a university Social Work course after he made comments on his personal Facebook page in support of biblical teaching on marriage and social ethics. Following a *Fitness to Practise Committee*

hearing at Sheffield University, second year Masters' student, Felix, has been told that he has been "excluded from further study on a programme leading to a professional qualification" and is "no longer recognized as a University student".'[5]

- A friend of mine, the late Gordon Wilson MP, was dismissed by Dundee Citizens Advice Bureau after he had criticized the Scottish Government's plan to re-define marriage.

But there is little need to multiply examples because it is all too evident around us, and the main question is that of whether we are going to be seduced by such anti-Christian pressure and turn our backs on Christ, or whether we can keep our focus and our faith on Jesus.

Interestingly, this same doubting Peter encouraged believers later with teaching about how to react when facing trials and pressure. We can summarize his advice in four sayings:

- Firstly, *don't be surprised.* He wrote, 'Beloved, do not be surprised at the fiery trial when it comes upon you to test you, as though something strange were happening to you' (1 Peter 4:12). He had heard Jesus being up-front about the opposition people might have to face if they would faithfully follow Him.
- Then secondly, *don't be depressed.* We were never promised that it would be easy to follow Christ or to stand up for Him.
- Then he says, *don't be ashamed.* 'If anyone suffers as a Christian, let him not be ashamed, but let him glorify God' (1 Peter 4:16).
- And fourthly, he says, *don't be paralysed.* 'Let those who suffer according to God's will entrust their souls to a faithful Creator while doing good' (1 Peter 4:19).

It's a great prescription for times *when doubts and fears arise*: do not be surprised, do not be depressed, do not be ashamed and do not be paralysed. After all, even if contemporary culture is hostile to Christianity, that does not affect the question of its truth.

Some of us have lived in a society which was at least nominally Christian. This is historically unusual; it is normal for Christians to feel under pressure from the world. The church has lived for most of its history in more or less alien cultures.

Jesus spoke famously about the cost of discipleship: 'If anyone would come after me, let him deny himself and take up his cross and follow me' (Matthew 16:24). These are words which would have sent a shiver down the spines of those who first heard them because, for them, taking up a cross was not a metaphor. The cross was a barbarous instrument of torture and suffering, and for us to refer to some minor thing as 'a cross we must bear' is probably quite inappropriate.

Christianity developed in a climate of opposition. On the one hand there was the pluralism of those who would take anything on board, but on the other hand there was the totalitarianism that simply would not tolerate anything like 'I am the way, and the truth, and the life' (John 14:6). In these early days, it must have seemed highly unlikely that Christianity could survive, much less grow and spread.

But it did, not by human power but because of the power of Christ.

We need to keep our eyes on Him. Hebrews emphasizes that. It says with wonderful simplicity, 'Consider Jesus' (Hebrews 3:1), and 'Let us fix our eyes on Jesus' (Hebrews 12:2 NIV).

The same is also true at the more personal level in relation to the storms and troubles of life that come sooner or later to everyone:

grief, illness, tragedy, disappointment and ultimately death. In times of stress, it is all too easy to doubt by focusing on the trouble rather than on the Lord, so that He might say to *us* also, 'Why did you doubt?'

### 'Lord, save me'

Peter's prayer in Matthew 14:30 must be one of the shortest prayers of the Bible and one of the shortest anyone could utter: 'Lord, save me.' Clearly it was not a time for fancy words or flowery expressions; he was in panic and fear.

God's Word assures us that even the shortest of prayers are heard.

And there is great encouragement in the word, 'immediately': 'Jesus immediately reached out his hand and took hold of him' (v. 31). The Bible assures us that Jesus stands ready to reach out to all who call to Him in sincerity and faith—not with a vague prayer like that of the sceptical Renan: 'O Lord, if there is a Lord, save my soul, if I have a soul.'[6] How different is the instruction in James 1:5–8:

> If any of you lacks wisdom, let him ask God, who gives generously to all without reproach, and it will be given him. But let him ask in faith, with no doubting, for the one who doubts is like a wave of the sea that is driven and tossed by the wind. For that person must not suppose that he will receive anything from the Lord; he is a double-minded man, unstable in all his ways.

As we have seen already, the word for *doubt* implies 'double mindedness'. It is the attitude that cannot make up its mind where it stands. Elijah challenged it in the great confrontation with the prophets of Baal at Mount Carmel; he asked, 'How long will you go limping between two different opinions? If the LORD is God, follow him; but if Baal, then follow him' (1 Kings 18:21).

There may be things we do not understand and cannot explain, but we do not need to know all the answers before we can trust in an almighty God. This narrative about Jesus walking on the water is contained in the same chapter as the record of John the Baptist's death—the man who had asked the question, 'Are you the one who is to come, or shall we look for another?' (Luke 7:19).

John, as we saw in the last chapter, was in prison precisely because he had declared God's truth, but we are not told of his reaction to Jesus' answer. And things got worse, as we read about the grim birthday party and Salome's probably sensuous dance which prompted Herod's crazy offer of any birthday gift for which she asked. Then follows the grisly account of John's head being brought in on a platter. We might well ask why—not *why Herodias had it in for John*, but *why God allowed it to happen*; *why didn't He step in to stay Herod's hand and save John's life as He saved Peter's here?*

It is the kind of question that has been asked time and time again through the centuries, and at the end of the day we simply do not know the answer. There are things that can be said about human freedom with all its potential for disastrous actions like this, but still we cannot explain everything and ultimately the question is, *'Is Jesus Christ to be trusted or not?'*

We can also add a factor which no other religion or philosophy can add—that God Himself has come right into our world of suffering and, because of Calvary, we know that He has plumbed its depths. Professor Tom Torrance expressed that aspect of the message of the cross when he wrote, 'If I did not believe in the cross, I could not believe in God. The cross means that, while there is no explanation of evil, God Himself has come into the midst of it in order to take it upon Himself, to triumph over it and deliver us from it.'[7]

Matthew 14:32–33 tells of Jesus and Peter getting back into the boat; the wind ceased 'and those in the boat worshipped him, saying, "Truly you are the Son of God".' Their faith was strengthened and they saw the reality of the Person of Christ—One who is the Lord of the wind and the waves (Mark 4:41), the One whose path was leading to the self-sacrifice of Calvary, the One of whom Romans 1:4 would say He 'was declared to be the Son of God in power according to the Spirit of holiness by his resurrection from the dead'.

We have considered His question to Peter, 'Why did you doubt?' It was because he paid more attention to the storm that surrounded him than to the Lord who had called him.

We may link with it an incident found in Mark 9 where Jesus miraculously healed a boy who had convulsions that made him fall about and foam at the mouth. The boy's father came to Jesus and said, 'If you can do anything, have compassion on us and help us.' Jesus responded, '"If you can"! All things are possible for one who believes', and the father said, 'I believe; help my unbelief!' It might be paraphrased, 'I do have faith; help me with regard to my unfaith.'

Peter's faith faltered, even as later his resolution faltered when he denied Jesus in the High Priest's courtyard (Mark 14:66–72). But when Jesus prophesied that denial, He also said, 'And when you have turned again, strengthen your brothers' (Luke 22:32).

Peter certainly did that. It is commonly believed that Mark, in writing the earliest of the Gospels, gained much of his material from

Peter, and we can imagine Peter telling of the incident on the lake and how he had learned to trust in Jesus even in the midst of the storm.

In 1 Peter 1, he wrote about the different experiences of life and how our faith can become stronger through testing. Quoting Peterson's paraphrase of Peter's words, 'Because Jesus was raised from the dead, we've been given a brand-new life and have everything to live for, including a future in heaven—and the future starts now!'[8]

'In this', Peter writes, 'you rejoice, though now for a little while, if necessary, you may have been grieved by various trials, so that the tested genuineness of your faith—more precious than gold that perishes though it is tested by fire—may be found to result in praise and glory and honour at the revelation of Jesus Christ. Though you have not seen him, you love him. Though you do not now see him, you believe in him and rejoice with joy that is inexpressible and filled with glory, obtaining the outcome of your faith, the salvation of your souls' (1 Peter 1:6–9).

Jesus' question to Peter was, 'Why did you doubt?' The answer, as we have seen, is that he paid more attention to the storm that surrounded him than to the Lord who had called him. The remedy is to reverse that and pay more attention to the Lord who calls us than to any storms that surround us.

## NOTES

1 *Strong's Exhaustive Concordance of the Bible* (Nashville: Crusade Bible Publishers, 1890).

2 *'Apologia'* is the Greek word which Peter used and it refers to a reasonable account of our faith. This is different from the common use of the word, apologetic, to suggest a diffident,

un-confident approach to something; apologetics has nothing to do with being apologetic about our faith in that sense. We cannot convert people by clever arguments; conversion is God's work (1 Corinthians 2:14). But we can, with His help, seek to remove some of the barriers and even challenge others' unbelief, seeking to demonstrate that, although we do not know all the answers to all the questions that can be asked, none of these questions are so big as to make Christianity incredible. May we be 'prepared to make a defence to anyone who asks you for a reason for the hope that is in you; yet do it with gentleness and respect' (1 Peter 3:15).

3   Guinness, Os, *Doubt*, (Berkhamsted, Lion Publishing, 1976), front cover.

4   *Evangelicals Now*, April 2016.

5   Ibid.

6   https://www.goodreads.com/quotes/103838-o-lord-if-there-is-a-lord-save-my-soul (accessed 14/09/23)

7   Torrance, Tom, *Preaching Christ Today*, (Grand Rapids: Eerdmans, 1996), p. 28.

8   Petersen, Eugene, *The Message*, p. 573.

# 10 'We had hoped ...'

## DOUBTS ABOUT THE VICTORY OF JESUS

To state the obvious, Christianity centres in Christ; the clue is in the name.

From any point of view, Jesus Christ is a massive figure in the world's history. Books continue to pour forth about Him; millions have followed Him; countless sermons have been preached about Him. A New Testament professor suggested that if a preacher should live to be 100, preaching twice every Sunday about Jesus, he would not be anywhere near the end of it. 'Any other subject under heaven would have been exhausted long ago; this theme remains bewilderingly rich, everlastingly fresh and fertile.'[1]

But what if doubts arise about Him—His person, His teaching, His miracles, the significance of His death or the reality of His resurrection?

For the two travellers described in Luke 24 there was a crushing sense of disappointment as they talked about Jesus. It was the afternoon of the day now known as Easter Day, and Cleopas and his companion walked the seven miles from Jerusalem to Emmaus in a mood of great despondency. They had had high hopes about Jesus but now they doubted it all. Their words, 'We had hoped ...' (Luke 24:21) describe their sad sense that it was all over.

The record does not say that they had succumbed to unbelief and, if it is true that doubt hovers somewhere between faith and unbelief, these two must have been very doubtful about (a) the message *of*

Jesus and (b) the message *about* Jesus. Perhaps they simply did not know what to think.

On the one hand there was the grim reality of all that had happened. In that terrible miscarriage of justice, Jesus had been hounded to a horrible death. Poor, weak Pilate had been manoeuvred into signing the death warrant, and Jesus was nailed to the cross. The physical agony must have been awful, and there were also the things that Jesus said while nailed up there—things like, 'Father, forgive them for they know not what they do' (Luke 23:34). That was mysterious, because the executioners knew pretty well what they were doing: they were carrying out the death penalty on a condemned man. Yet Jesus said there was something going on that they did not know or understand.

Then there was his cry: 'It is finished' (John 19:30), which had not sounded like a weary surrender to a finally welcome death; it had sounded more like a cry of triumph. What could it all mean?

And there was also His word to one of the other two men crucified that day: 'Today you will be with me in Paradise' (Luke 23:43). What on earth could it all mean?

But it all came to an end. Jesus breathed His last and His body was taken down and laid in a tomb with a great stone covering the entrance.

All of that was on one side of the equation. Yet Luke tells us that, as the two people walked, 'they were talking with each other about all these things that had happened' (Luke 24:14), and when the unrecognized Stranger joined them and asked what had been happening, they spoke about Jesus as 'a prophet mighty in deed and word before God and all the people' (24:19).

They could not get that out of their minds either. There had been amazing happenings—like the calming of the storm, the feeding of five thousand people with an apparently small picnic lunch, and even people being raised from the dead. And there had been all His teaching, wonderful and unforgettable words of love and grace. They regarded Him as a prophet, which could signify 'merely a prophet' and not more than that, or perhaps they were thinking of the Old Testament's messianic prophecy to Moses: 'I will raise up for them a prophet like you from among their brothers' (Deuteronomy 18:18). Had they come to see Jesus as the fulfilment of such prophecies?

Then there is the phrase about the hopes that had been raised by Jesus' life and ministry. 'We had hoped that he was the one to redeem Israel' (Luke 24:21). Many people looked for, and longed for, a political deliverer, a warrior Messiah, who would drive out the Roman occupation and establish freedom for Israel, but there was probably more than that in Cleopas' words. They had hoped that He would bring a redemption greater still—redemption from the power of sin and the fear of death. Had Jesus not spoken about giving His life 'as a ransom for many' (Mark 10:45)?

And now, with His crucifixion, it seemed as if all of that had faded away. That expression, 'we had hoped', speaks of great expectations, but how could they hold on to any such hopes now? That was their dilemma and their sadness.

Then, as they talked about such things, the risen Jesus 'drew near and went with them. But their eyes were kept from recognizing him' (Luke 24:15–16). And if we were to say, *'How on earth could they have Jesus Himself walking beside them and not recognize Him?'*—well, obviously, they knew that Jesus was dead and buried, and you do not expect dead people to be joining you as you walk along the road. Whoever the Stranger was, it would never have occurred to them that it could possibly be Jesus.

## In all the Scriptures

Later, Jesus spoke and we are told, 'Beginning with Moses and all the Prophets, he interpreted to them in all the Scriptures the things concerning himself' (v. 27).

After Jesus had left them, Cleopas and his companion said to each other, 'Did not our hearts burn within us while he talked to us on the road, while he opened to us the Scriptures?' (v. 32). Here came the first doubts about their doubts—their gloomy conclusion that the dream was over and everything had ended in failure. That had been their mood, and as they engaged in this travelling Bible study, a ray of light shone into their darkness. He showed them how it had all been prophesied that 'the Christ should suffer these things and enter into his glory' (v. 26).

That later phrase, 'Did not our hearts burn within us', tells us of the dawning of a new hope. Their doubts about the whole Jesus phenomenon were being called into question; they began to doubt any conclusion that it was all over.

There was another factor that was causing further ripples of confusion and doubt. They explained to the Stranger, 'Some women of our company amazed us. They were at the tomb early in the morning, and when they did not find his body, they came back saying that they had even seen a vision of angels who said that he was alive' (vv. 22–23).

All of these things—their talk about all that had happened, their reference to the Prophet, their 'we had hoped', the experience of their hearts burning at the opening of the Scriptures, and the rumours spread by the women's reports—must have put the two into a spin. What did it all add up to? What could it all mean? Was there still hope?

In an earlier chapter, we referred to G. K. Chesterton's experience of being 'visited by the first wild doubts about doubt'[2]. James S. Stewart referred to the same kind of thing in a televised conversation, in which he spoke about being 'disillusioned with disillusionment'.[3]

If Cleopas and his friend had become disillusioned about the seemingly abortive Christian movement, these events caused them to be disillusioned with that disillusionment; perhaps there was hope after all.

## The dawning of hope

And indeed there was! The greatest miracle of all had happened: the very Jesus who had been so undoubtedly put to death was undoubtedly alive again. In verse 31, 'Their eyes were opened, and they recognized him.' The Stranger was not a stranger; it was the Lord. And this Easter faith was established once and for all—the faith that would make all the difference to countless generations of people who have had their doubts dissolved in the wonderful reality.

It is a realization that dawns on people in different ways. A minister in Birmingham was in his study, actually preparing an Easter sermon, when it dawned on him. He tells of putting down his pen and pacing up and down the room. '"Christ is alive," I said to myself. It came upon me with a burst of glory. It was to me a new discovery. I thought all along I had believed it, but not until that day, did I feel sure about it.'[4]

Or again, the once-cynical Malcolm Muggeridge spoke about this very story of the Emmaus Road in connection with a film series he was making in the Holy Land:

> I finished off my filming in the Holy Land by taking, with a friend, the road to Emmaus. As my friend and I walked along, like Cleopas and his friend, we recalled as they did the events of the crucifixion and its aftermath in the light of our utterly different and yet similar world. Nor was it a fancy that we too were joined by a third Presence. And I tell you that wherever the walk and whoever the wayfarers, there is always this third Presence ready to emerge from the shadows and fall in step along the dusty, stony way.[5]

For the Emmaus Road two, it was through the Bible study and then the breaking of bread that the reality of the presence of that risen Lord dawned upon them.

Was there ever a Bible study like it? 'Beginning with Moses and all the Prophets, he interpreted to them in all the Scriptures the things concerning himself' (v. 27). If only we could have been flies on the wall of that room! There was Jesus opening it all up to them—the real meaning and significance of the things written down centuries beforehand, all pointing to Him.

This expression we have emphasized—'Did not our hearts burn within us while he talked to us on the road'—it happened 'while he opened to us the Scriptures' (Luke 24:32). And this holds the clue to the resolution of many of our doubts. Instead of allowing doubts to drive us away from the Bible and from the fellowship of God's people gathered around the Bible, the best thing is to look again at this book which is the inspired Word of God.

A well-known hymn says, 'O what peace we often forfeit, O what needless pain we bear, all because we do not carry everything to God in prayer'[6]. The same could be said about our questions and doubts; bring them to God in His Word. This, after all, is no dead letter or dry-as-dust book about ancient history; nor is it only a manual for living which may be relevant enough but not very exciting. Rather, this is the living Word of God. It is 'living and active' (Hebrews 4:12), and it brings light (Psalm 119:130). This is what happened on the Emmaus Road.

## Hearts strangely warmed

The experience encapsulated in the phrase, 'Did not our hearts burn within us', is one that has been replicated millions of times as the truth has dawned upon people's hearts and minds. With some it has come as the sudden revelation of something they had never previously considered; with others it may be that something, already believed, dawns upon them afresh.

It may happen in a so-called mountain-top experience when everything is wonderful and nothing seems more natural than to believe in the living Lord, or it may be even in some time of trouble or stress—situations in which some people turn *away* from the way of faith; yet even in that time of trouble, it all becomes more real than ever.

That is how it was with Job who, after his many trials and torments, said, 'I had heard of you by the hearing of the ear, but now my eye sees you' (Job 42:5).

This is the time when faith shifts over from being a theoretical and maybe even lamely accepted thing and becomes instead something vital and alive.

The Emmaus Road two had experienced huge disappointment; it seemed as if their hopes had been dashed. And how many people are there who could be described in the same terms: people who once had some kind of faith but things happened and that faith, which once seemed to hold great possibilities, became a forgotten and maybe even shattered thing.

For some, faith has been threatened by the notion that science has displaced religion, although we should really speak about scient*ism*—the notion that everything can be explained by physical science. For others, it may be a kind of psychological pressure of the idea that faith in God is simply a device for psychologically immature people, a crutch, or even Karl Marx's famous 'opium of the people'.

For others, doubt is an even more intensely personal thing. They have suffered some sad experience in life or possibly watched someone else be struck down by some cruel blow. There is much that can and should be said about such things[7], but the main thing is to realize and know that God understands. As the hymn says:

> Though now ascended up on high,
> he sees us with a brother's eye'
> he shares with us the human name
> and knows the frailty of our frame.

Our fellow-sufferer yet retains
a fellow-feeling for our pains,
and still remembers in the skies
his tears, his agonies and cries.

In all that pains the human heart,
the Man of Sorrows had a part;
he sympathizes with our grief
and to the sufferer sends relief.[8]

'We do not have a high priest who is unable to sympathize with our weaknesses, but one who in every respect has been tempted as we are, yet without sin. Let us then with confidence draw near to the throne of grace, that we may receive mercy and find grace to help in time of need' (Hebrews 4:15–16).

Cleopas and his companion found renewed faith and hope as Jesus opened the Scriptures to them (v. 27) and opened their eyes to understand the Scriptures (v. 45), but the actual moment of recognition seems to have come at the table when 'he took the bread and blessed and broke it and gave it to them' (v. 30). Perhaps they suddenly saw the scars on his hands or wrists, or was it His voice as He spoke these words? Whatever be the case, it was as if the veil was lifted from their eyes and they could see clearly that this was not a stranger who happened to be surprisingly ignorant about all that had been going on in those days. 'Their eyes were opened, and they recognized him' (v. 31).

Then, as with His other resurrection appearances when He appeared suddenly and then disappeared, so on this occasion also—

He suddenly dis-appeared, His risen body being the same and yet different.

The two friends rushed back to Jerusalem to tell the others. Daylight may be fading around them, but in their hearts light had dawned, the light of a brilliant day that will never end.

## Abide with me

One other detail of the story is particularly interesting. Luke tells us (vv. 28–29), 'So they drew near to the village to which they were going. He acted as if he were going farther, but they urged him strongly, saying, "Stay with us, for it is toward evening and the day is now far spent." So he went in to stay with them.' (The words, 'with them', may indicate that the two walkers were husband and wife.)

In poetic form, it reads, 'Abide with me; fast falls the eventide'; the hymn that has been sung so many, many times as people have sought comfort in its familiar words—hackneyed in some ways because of constant repetition, yet profound words of faith. Henry Frances Lyte had visited a dying friend. One version of the story says he had read to him this twenty-fourth chapter of Luke's gospel. The friend kept repeating the phrase, 'Abide with us' and this became the inspiration behind the hymn which has become one of the most well-known hymns in the English language.

> I need Thy presence every passing hour;
> What but Thy grace can foil the tempter's power.
> Who like thyself my guide and stay can be?
> Through cloud and sunshine, O abide with me.

I fear no foe with Thee at hand to bless;
Ills have no weight and tears no bitterness;
Where is death's sting? Where, grace, thy victory?
I triumph still if Thou abide with me.[9]

Their doubts had been overcome. Through the Bible study and the breaking of the bread they had come to know the Jesus who was and is still alive—the Jesus who does not force Himself on anyone, as signified by the words, 'as if he were going farther'. He awaited their invitation, as He does ours.

## NOTES

1  James S. Stewart, quoted in a letter of Stephen Olford, Easter 1982.

2  Chesterton, C. K., *Orthodoxy*, (Dover Publications edition, 2004), p. 77.

3  Television programme, *Why I Believe*, published in print by St. Ninian's Crieff Book Department in 1963.

4  Dale, R. W., quoted in: Gunn, G. S., *The Indispensable Christ*, (London: James Clarke, 1962), p. 186f.

5  Muggeridge, Malcolm, *Another King*, (Edinburgh: Saint Andrew Press, 1968), p. 13.

6  Hymn, 'What a Friend we have in Jesus', by Joseph Scriven, 1820–86.

7  I have written on the subject in: *Is Christianity Credible in a Suffering World?*—the first of the Solas Papers, to be found at: https://www.solas-cpc.org/wp-content/uploads/2017/11/The-Solas-Papers-edition-1-Nov-13.pdf

8  Michael Bruce, 1746–67. In: *Praise! Book*, No. 501.

9  Hymn, 'Abide with me', by Henry Francis Lyte, 1793–1847.

# 11 Seeing and believing

## DOUBTS ABOUT THE REALITY OF THE RESURRECTION

In the last chapter, we considered the two disciples who were devastated by the death of Jesus and then met the risen Lord. But there is one disciple whose name is for ever linked with doubt about whether Jesus really had risen from the dead—the one known through the ages as 'doubting Thomas'.

His assertion, 'Unless I see … I will never believe', sounds like the attitude of many people of our time: people who would claim to have a matter of fact and even scientific view, who would dismiss 'religion' as make-belief and dreams, and who would say they'll only believe what can be seen and proved.

They would claim to be very modern and rational in their thinking, although when you think about it there is something rather strange in talking about only believing what can be seen and proved, since we might ask, 'How could you do otherwise if it visible and proven?'

But, of course, it is not, originally, the expression of twenty-first-century scepticism but the response of Thomas to reports that Jesus had risen from the dead. He said, 'Unless I see in his hands the mark of the nails, and place my finger in the mark of the nails, and place my hand into his side, I will never believe' (John 20:25).

Thomas seems to have been a person of gloomy temperament, a 'glass-half-empty' kind of man. In terms of the old rhyme about two men looking through the same prison bars, one seeing mud, the other stars, Thomas was probably the kind to look downwards and see the mud.

But his inclusion in the Bible and among the disciples is a great encouragement because it makes clear that Jesus has time for those who share Thomas' temperament. He accepts not only the extrovert Peter, but also the gloomy and sceptical Thomas (not to mention Matthew with his background of questionable honesty, James and John who had weird ideas about greatness in God's kingdom and the other Simon who had been part of a guerrilla organisation).

Thomas' inclusion reminds us that the people of the Bible did not always find faith easy. Especially if we are inclined to look on previous generations with the kind of chronological snobbery that assumes we today are so much cleverer and more sophisticated, we can be thankful for Thomas' inclusion.

The record tells us that he was not present when Jesus first appeared to the disciples on the evening of what we now call Easter Day. The other disciples told him that they had seen the Lord—and what was Thomas' response? Did he say, 'Oh, how wonderful,' or 'Thank you for sharing this wonderful news with me,' or 'That's tremendous, to know that Calvary was not the end? Not at all; Thomas' reaction was one of complete scepticism.

It was a week later when Jesus appeared to them again and we might imagine the others, during that week, trying to convince Thomas that they had not been dreaming or pretending; the very Jesus they knew had appeared in front of them, alive again.

And did Thomas entertain doubts about his own doubts during these days, or did he continue to say what he had said on that first Sunday? One might even imagine one of the disciples saying to him,

*'Thomas, don't you want to believe it?'* and Thomas responding, *'Of course I want to believe it, but wanting to believe something doesn't make it true.'*

The hard-headed attitude of Thomas must have persisted through that week until 'Eight days later, his disciples were inside again, and Thomas was with them' (John 20:26). Presumably he did not expect anything remarkable to happen; would he even have anticipated making a 'told you so' statement to the others? He probably expected to be saying to them, *'We just have to accept that it's all over. No flights of visionary fancy are going to change things.'*

There is a conversation in a novel in which one character is questioning another about his religious beliefs. The dialogue is as follows:

> 'But, my dear Sebastian, you can't seriously believe it all?'
> 'Can't I?'
> 'I mean, about Christmas and the star and the three kings and the ox and the ass?'
> 'O yes, I believe all that. It's a lovely idea.'
> 'But you can't believe things because they're a lovely idea.'
> 'But I do. That's how I believe.'[1]

Well, that certainly is not how Thomas believed things; he needed something more than *nice ideas*.

And the truth is that everything told against Thomas being convinced of the resurrection: the undeniable fact that Jesus was dead and buried; the knowledge that dead people do not appear again; the personality of Thomas. He probably thought that the others had deluded themselves into believing, or that gullibility had produced the notion of the resurrection.

The idea that faith is the outcome of a kind of desperate longing that it should all be true is a persistent one, yet it flies in the face of the fact that, although the Bible's message brings immense comfort and solace, it can also be decidedly *un*comfortable and *un*welcome. This is why the renowned believer, C. S. Lewis, described his conversion in terms of a reluctant surrender: 'That which I greatly feared had at last come upon me, ... I gave in, and admitted that God was God, and knelt and prayed: perhaps, that night, the most dejected and reluctant convert in all England.'[2]

The same point was made by a one-time Principal of Aberdeen University when he suggested, 'Those who take the Bible seriously know that where the God of the Bible is concerned, men search for Him in precisely the way that the average mouse searches for the average cat!'[3]

He was concerned to refute the idea that faith is the result of wishful thinking; in fact, he turned the tables on this assertion:

> There is no more false piece of sentimentality than the statement that we needs must love the highest when we see it. Quite often we hate it, and we hate it because it is a rebuke to our pride and self-sufficiency. If we have wronged it, we hate it even more. Accordingly the natural unregenerate man has no love to God, indeed the Scriptures with their usual realism tell us plainly that the carnal mind is enmity towards God. ... With what eagerness we all clutch at these explanations (Oedipus complex etc) which explain away our sense of responsibility! This is why atheism has a perennial appeal; it is wishful thinking in its most enticing form.[4]

So, he turned the tables on the notion that Christianity is simply wishful thinking and that it flies in the face of the facts. Consider, for example, the apostle Paul; his story shows what a fallacy it is to think that Christianity is a placebo to give its followers a quiet life. After his conversion, and because of it, Paul had anything but a quiet life. He was beset by one problem after another: persecution, hardships, trials, being chased from one place to another and, almost certainly, eventual martyrdom. If Paul had wanted an easy life, he should have tried some other way.

Far from the way of faith leading to an easy life, it is often the opposite. Was it not faith that led David Livingstone to undergo all the deprivations and difficulties that faced him as a missionary and explorer in central Africa? Was it not commitment to Christ that led Dietrich Bonhoeffer to stand against the despotism of Hitler even at the cost of his own life? Is it not faith that leads many people in China and Pakistan and other countries to stand up for Jesus, even at great personal sacrifice and cost?

No, the way of faith is not the result of wishful thinking; anything but!

This is not to overlook the enormous blessings of faith in Christ. The gospel claim is that it is Christ who gives peace and fulfilment in abundant measure—life in all its fullness here (John 10:10) and pleasures for evermore at his right hand (Psalm 16:11). The glories of the gospel far outweigh the 'threat'.

Peter would write later about the inexpressible joy (1 Peter 1:8) that God gives to His people. This passage has been vividly paraphrased by Eugene Peterson:

What a God we have! And how fortunate we are to have him, this Father of our Master Jesus! Because Jesus was raised from the dead, we've been given a brand-new life and have everything to live for, including a future in heaven—and the future starts now! God is keeping careful watch over us and the future. The Day is coming when you'll have it all—life healed and whole. I know how great this makes you feel, even though you have to put up with every kind of aggravation in the meantime.[5]

Thomas has traditionally been known as 'Doubting Thomas'—not in the Bible but across the generations. But history has been unkind to him; he might more appropriately be known as 'loyal Thomas' because this is a disciple who was faithful, even though he was inclined to look on the dark side of things and was perhaps pessimistic by nature.

When we put together the few references in Scripture to Thomas, we find several stages in the story of his faith. In John 11, we see courageous faith; in John 14, we see confused faith; in John 19, we see crushed faith; and then in John 20, there is convinced faith.

## Courageous faith

His courageous faith is seen (or heard) in John 11:16, where Thomas said to his fellow disciples, 'Let us also go, that we may die with him.' They were in Bethany, which was not far from Jerusalem and, in Bethany, Lazarus had died: the man whom Jesus was going to raise from the dead in an amazing demonstration of His authority over death. In verse 7 Jesus says, 'Let us go to Judea again,' and naturally the disciples protested. They pointed out that it was not long since people had wanted to stone Him to death there.

And it was when Jesus insisted on His plan that Thomas spoke up. It is one of only a few occasions when we have his words. He said, 'Let us also go, that we may die with him.' Thomas could see no good coming of it, but he was all for sticking with Jesus, nonetheless. Is that a doubting Thomas or a loyal Thomas?

He does seem to have had a gloomy temperament; recruitment agencies might not have recommended him for a position among the twelve disciples, just as they would probably have discounted Matthew because of questions about his previous honesty in business, Peter as far too volatile and Judas as too greedy.

We see his gloomy temperament in this first incident, along with his gritty loyalty. He realized that going back to Judea was tantamount to putting their heads into the lion's mouth, *but* if Jesus was determined to do it, and even though Thomas could only see it ending in catastrophe, he expressed this determination to stick with Jesus regardless, and he sought to encourage the others to do the same. 'Let us also go'— *Yes and die with him if that's how this is all going to end.*

His was a courageous faith. And it is a challenge to the feeble faith that runs away when there is opposition to Jesus and His way—the kind of vague religion that tends, when the pressure is on, to hold back or run away. Thomas could well have been the subject who sat for Bunyan's portrait of the dedicated and loyal Christian, when he wrote (in its original wording):

> Who would true valour see,
> Let him come hither;
> One here will constant be,
> Come wind, come weather.

> There's no discouragement
> Shall make him once relent
> His first avowed intent
> To be a pilgrim.[6]

## Confused faith

When we fast-forward to John 14, we come to a passage that has been a favourite one for many people: words of great encouragement and comfort, especially in the face of the last enemy.

It is the passage where Jesus speaks about the many rooms in the Father's house, where He utters the famous, 'I am the way, and the truth, and the life' (v. 6), and where He speaks about giving His people a peace that the world cannot give or take away.

And in verse 4, He says to the disciples, 'You know the way to where I am going.' It is wonderful for us to consider this after all these centuries of reflection on the words and with all that we know of the whole ministry, death and resurrection of Jesus. But when the words were first spoken, they must have sounded very mysterious.

Perhaps we can, in our imaginations, picture the disciples looking around at one another with puzzled expressions on their faces, or perhaps blank looks of incomprehension. And it was Thomas who came out with it. He was the one who would say what the others may have been thinking but would not say: 'Lord, we do not know where you are going. How can we know the way?' (v. 5). He was not prepared to stay shtum—to make it look as if they were all understanding Jesus' words when in fact, they had not a clue what He was talking about.

And it was in response to that question from Thomas that Jesus uttered his famous words, 'I am the way, and the truth, and the life.'

Thomas' words are not so much the expression of doubt as of incomprehension, and it is another incidental reminder that we can bring our questions and puzzles to Jesus. There may be some people to whom you would be afraid to open your heart or confess your guilt—or admit your inability to understand—but here is a Friend to whom you can bring anything at all. He did not turn on Thomas and rebuke him for his obtuseness.

We are assured that Jesus does not dismiss us in our denseness. We are talking about the sympathizing Jesus who does not break the bruised reed or snuff out the faintly burning wick (Isaiah 42:3)—a prophecy which Matthew sees as fulfilled in the ministry of Jesus (Matthew 12:20).

This is a Lord to whom we can open our hearts without fear of rejection. We are invited to come just as we are, even if (in the words of a hymn that has been quoted already) 'tossed about with many a conflict, many a doubt'.[7]

## Crushed faith

John 19 describes the events leading up to the crucifixion of Jesus and then the dire event itself. Thomas is not mentioned in the chapter but we can be sure that his courageous (even if sometimes confused) faith would be shattered.

True, Jesus had tried to prepare them for what lay ahead; Matthew 16:21 says, 'From that time Jesus began to show his disciples that he must go to Jerusalem and suffer many things from the elders and chief priests and scribes, and be killed, and on the third day be raised.' On at least three other occasions he forewarned them (Matthew 17:22–23; 20:17–19; 26:2). On one occasion we are specifically told (Mark 9:32), 'But they did not understand the saying, and were afraid to ask him.'

And when it happened, they were shocked, baffled and shattered. It must have seemed like the nemesis of everything—the extinction of all hopes that in Jesus a new day might have been dawning. To see *anyone* crucified must have been a dreadful thing; to see this Man crucified—how utterly dreadful. Whatever faith and hopes Thomas and the others had, these hopes had now been dashed.

And that brings us back to John 20:24 and the simple statement, 'Now Thomas, one of the Twelve, called the Twin, was not with them when Jesus came,'—'one of the Twelve' indeed, even with his gloomy temperament and tendency to see the dark side of things.

'When Jesus came' refers to the most stupendous miracle of all. It is such a staggering thing that many sceptics have tried to think out and 'explain' what 'really' happened! They start from the premise that it could not have been as Matthew, Mark, Luke and John tell it—it must be a made-up story, whether from people who were themselves conned or from people who set out to con others.

However, there are certain aspects of the story which would have been quite different if any of them *had* made it up:

- First of all, it would have centred on eye-witness accounts of the actual event of the resurrection, whereas the gospels give no account of the event itself. None of the disciples were present to see Christ when He got up and exited the tomb. A fabricator would surely have plugged that gap.
- If anyone had been making up this story, he would have been

very careful about who were said to be the witnesses of the risen Jesus, and no-one would have faked the first witness to be a woman (John 20:14)! In that culture, at that time, a woman's testimony was not considered binding.

- Thirdly, a fabricator would probably have published his account far from the place where it was all supposed to have happened, whereas belief in the resurrection originated in the very city where Jesus was crucified.
- Another factor is that the four gospel accounts of the resurrection are not easy to fit together into a chronological sequence. If the story had been made up, its tellers would have made sure that they ironed out all potential puzzles.
- The narrators, if making up a story, would surely have painted a sympathetic picture of the perpetrators of the myth. The account of Peter's denials of Christ, for example, would have been omitted, and as for 'doubting Thomas'—better to exclude that from the story!
- Sixthly, a made-up story would have discouraged any investigation; it might even have pronounced dire threats against anyone who would pry into the details. One of the remarkable things about Paul's list of resurrection witnesses is his assertion that many of the 500 people who said they saw the risen Jesus (1 Corinthian 15:6) were 'still alive'. This is tantamount to saying, *'If you don't believe me, you can go and ask them for yourself.'*
- Lastly, people who knew the whole thing was a made-up story would stop short of dying for their story; under threat they would recant and own up to their deception. The truth is that

many of these eyewitnesses held to their story in the teeth of torture and execution.

There are many other factors about the evidence for the resurrection—notably the fact that nobody produced a dead body (though many had a vested interest in doing so), the change in the disciples and the existence of the church—and these factors can be checked out elsewhere.[8]

But the disciples, including Thomas, were convinced that this miracle of all miracles had really happened. It changed everything, as Paul would draw out in 1 Corinthians 15. There, he wrote about how, without it, there would be no forgiveness, no faith and no future: 'If Christ has not been raised, then our preaching is in vain and your faith is in vain ... your faith is futile and you are still in your sins. Then those also who have fallen asleep in Christ have perished' (1 Corinthians 15:14, 17–18).

'But in fact,' he goes on, 'Christ has been raised from the dead, the firstfruits of those who have fallen asleep' (v. 20), and then towards the end of the chapter, 'Thanks be to God, who gives us the victory through our Lord Jesus Christ' (v. 57).

James Philip used a simple illustration to describe the effects of Christ's resurrection:

> When we put on an electric switch, a current of some 240 volts passes into the bulb whose filament is strong enough to hold the current captive and therefore lights up. But if a current of 19,000 volts is passed through, it will blow the filament, bulb and all, to smithereens! This is how it is in the spiritual realm. When mortal man, by reason of his sin, passes into death, death holds him captive; but when this Man—the second Adam, the Lord of nature, sickness,

devils and death—enters death, death itself is destroyed, and all that is held captive by it is released.[9]

All of that is contained in this little phrase: 'When Jesus came.' It was the most amazing and wonderful thing for the disciples—all ten of them. Everyone knows about Judas, but Thomas also missed it! He was absent when Jesus appeared.

Where was he? Nobody knows. Perhaps he was wandering about in a daze, trying to come to terms with the misery of this defeat, that which all along he had felt was bound to happen. And how was he to live down the shame of it? He and the others had committed themselves to the Teacher from Nazareth and now they would simply have to hope that the dust would settle, the storm pass and things get back to normal once again. It had been an exciting adventure, but it was all over.

John 20:26 begins, 'Eight days later'. What a long week that must have been! Did the others, when they spoke to Thomas, try to persuade him that Jesus really had risen and appeared to them? *It was no hallucination or dream—we were there and we saw Him with our own eyes.'*

And when Thomas still expressed his ingrained scepticism, perhaps they would say to him, 'Well, at least make sure you're with us this coming Sunday.'

Perhaps reluctantly, Thomas was present—probably not expecting anything to happen. But John records, 'Although the doors were locked, Jesus came and stood among them and said, "Peace be with you."'

## Convinced faith

And then—wonder of wonders - He was speaking directly to Thomas in particular, offering the visible, tangible proof Thomas had demanded. And what did He say? 'Put your finger here and see my hands; and put out your hand and place it in my side. Do not disbelieve but believe' (v. 27).

That does not mean *'suspend your judgement, just swallow hard and take a leap in the dark'*. We are to use our minds and our rational powers to think things out, but there comes a point when He says to us (as NIV translates it), 'Stop doubting and believe.' Jesus' challenge, through the Word of Scripture and the ministry of the Holy Spirit, is to move from unbelief and doubt to faith.

It happened with Thomas. This disciple, who had demanded the proof of sight and touch responded: 'My Lord and my God!' It is one of the most fulsome expressions of faith to be found in the whole of Scripture—and it comes from the lips of someone known to history as 'doubting Thomas'.

'Lord' in Greek is the word, *kurios*—the very word which the Greek Old Testament used for the name of Yahweh, the name of the eternal triune God. And here is Thomas addressing it to the risen Jesus.

The fact that the doubts of this particular disciple were overcome is one piece of strong evidence for the truth of the resurrection—and not merely as some kind of ethereal or 'spiritual' happening, but as an actual event, for Thomas was a man who was anything but gullible or suggestible.

There have been many who have suggested that the inner core of Christian belief is to be found in some 'spiritual and personal' resurrection—that somehow His presence seemed to be still with them and although His body lay a-mouldering in the grave, his soul goes marching on.

That is not what Christianity is about. It is rather about faith in and a growing relationship with that Lord who 'presented himself alive to them after his suffering by many proofs, appearing to them during forty days and speaking about the kingdom of God' (Acts 1:3), and who was 'declared to be the Son of God in power according to the Spirit of holiness by his resurrection from the dead, Jesus Christ our Lord' (Romans 1:4).

John, in writing this record, made the point that the whole Gospel had been written with that intention: that others might come to the same faith. Out of all the things that could have been selected and included in his twenty-one chapters, these things have been recorded 'so that you [the reader] may believe that Jesus is the Christ, the Son of God, and that by believing you may have life in his name' (John 20:31).

That sounds as if it could have been the final word of John's Gospel, although there is in fact another chapter—a chapter of more resurrection appearances—before it ends with a similar note about how there would not be room in the whole world for everything that could be written about Jesus. But all of the things God wants us to know *are* here in the Bible, written down, under the guidance of the Spirit, that we might have and hold to this faith in Jesus as 'the Christ, the Son of God' and have life in His name.

'Doubting Thomas'? 'Believing Thomas' would be better. Here is one in whom we see:

- courageous faith—in that he would go forward with Jesus even if it meant suffering and death.

- confused faith—in a man who was prepared to bring his questions and his confusion to Jesus.
- crushed faith—as he saw this Lord nailed to the cross to die.
- convinced faith—as he bowed before the risen Lord with his declaration, 'My Lord and my God.'

Obviously, we cannot see Jesus in the same way as Thomas did, yet we are challenged to put our faith in Him even though we have not seen Him, and so to be among those addressed later by Peter: 'Though you have not seen him, you love him. Though you do not now see him, you believe in him and rejoice with joy that is inexpressible and filled with glory, obtaining the outcome of your faith, the salvation of your souls' (1 Peter 1:8–9).

The fact that the doubts of Thomas were overcome is one evidence for the truth of the resurrection and encourages us to believe it and confide in this risen Lord. Verse 29 of John 20 has Jesus' last beatitude, with an eye to all who would believe because of the testimony of Thomas and the others. 'Have you believed because you have seen me? Blessed are those who have not seen and yet have believed.'

That is His Word of blessing for us, for all who share Thomas' faith in this presently unseen Lord who promises His believing people, 'I go to prepare a place for you' (John 14:2), and 'Because I live, you also will live' (John 14:19).

### NOTES

1  Waugh, Evelyn, *Brideshead Revisited*, (London: Penguin Books edition, 1960; originally published 1945), p. 78.

2  Lewis, C. S., *Surprised by Joy*, (London: Fontana Books, 1955), p. 182.

3  Taylor, Sir Thomas, *Where One Man Stands*, (Edinburgh: St Andrew Press, 1960), p. 84.

4  Ibid., p. 24.

5  Peterson, Eugene, *The Message*, (Colorado Springs: Navpress, 1993), p. 572.

6  From Part 2 of *The Pilgrim's Progress* by John Bunyan, 1628–88 (Harmondsworth: Penguin edition of 1965), p. 354.

7  From the hymn, 'Just as I am', by Charlotte Elliott, 1789–1871.

8  For example, chapter 4 of John Stott's *Basic Christianity* (published by IVP). Two interesting investigations come from people who started out as unbelievers but were convinced by the evidence. One is a lawyer, Frank Morison, who wrote *Who Moved The Stone?* first published in 1930 by Faber & Faber. The other is a journalist, Lee Strobel, who has written *The Case for Christ*, (published in 1998 by Zondervan).

9  Philip, James, *The Death and Resurrection of Christ* (undated transcript of sermon preached in Holyrood Abbey Church, Edinburgh).

# 12 What? Now?

## DOUBTS ABOUT THE URGENCY OF GOD'S MESSAGE

'I f Christianity is true, why do the majority of intelligent people not believe it?'

This is a question that may have occurred to many people, and the late Paul Little responded, 'The answer is precisely the same as the reason the majority of unintelligent people don't believe it. They don't want to because they're unwilling to accept the moral demands it would make on their lives.'[1]

That is blunt, but perhaps it gets to the heart of many people's rejection of Christianity. Even if all their questions could be answered and all the causes of their doubts cleared up, they still would not follow Jesus—because they basically just do not want to.

And often they do not want to because it would be too disturbing and too demanding. They realize that, if they were to take Christ and Christianity seriously, it would mean changes in their lives and they are not prepared to make such changes—in particular, to give up things they know would not square with Christian commitment.

This is a different kind of doubt from the others we have considered. This concerns people who ask questions not really to find out the answers but to avoid the challenge to commitment.

That is what Paul Little was meaning: with some people it is not a matter of high or low intelligence but of whether they are willing to face the challenges of the truth. They have a vested interest in being doubters, because to do otherwise would make demands on them that they are not prepared to face.

This is not a sweeping dismissal of all doubt, of course. There *are* people who are held back by genuine doubt and where there are genuine and honest doubts, it is important that there should be people willing to follow the admonition of 1 Peter 3:15: 'In your hearts honour Christ the Lord as holy, always being prepared to make a defence to anyone who asks you for a reason for the hope that is in you; yet do it with gentleness and respect.' No one is going to be won by scorn or arrogance—the attitude that dismisses all doubt as silly or assumes that *all* doubt is simply evasion and prejudiced rejection of belief.

But still, there is also this kind of doubt, and it too is something that is seen in the Bible—in the case of a Roman governor called Felix, a man of power who had the opportunity of hearing the Christian message from the apostle Paul.

Felix was intrigued by it, attracted to some degree by this new message and perhaps impressed by the zeal of Paul. But he did not want to face up to the truth for the simple reason that there were issues in his life that he was unwilling to change. Believing would have meant changes and, as has been said often, it is easy to raise doubts about things we do not want to think or do.

There is an unusually frank description of such an attitude in the case of the writer, Aldous Huxley, who wrote about his rejection of faith:

> For myself, as, no doubt, for most of my contemporaries, the philosophy of meaninglessness was essentially an instrument of liberation. The liberation we desired was simultaneously liberation

from a certain political and economic system and liberation from a certain system of morality. We objected to the morality because it interfered with our sexual freedom; we objected to the political and economic system because it was unjust. The supporters of these systems claimed that in some way they embodied the meaning (a Christian meaning, they insisted) of the world. There was one admirably simple method of confuting these people and at the same time justifying ourselves in our political and erotic revolt: we could deny that the world has any meaning whatsoever.[2]

Now, in the 2020s, we face a situation where many people actually regard Christianity, and its moral teaching in particular, as not only unpalatable but wrong and unacceptable. Whereas once the Ten Commandments would have been seen by almost everyone as a good and desirable prescription for living, now, 'To suggest the Ten Commandments form the bedrock of society is unjust and immoral. People are rejecting Christianity not because faith in God is intellectually impossible but because the God of the Bible is morally repugnant.'[3]

And we are faced with the question of whether to bow to such political correctness, which is rather different in practice from biblical correctness. Is it tenable any longer to hold to out-of-fashion ideas such as the view that marriage can only be between one man and one woman or the view that the unborn have a right to be protected in the womb. Or should we simply surrender and go with the flow of contemporary values?

## Felix

Acts 24 tells the story of Felix. He was the governor of the Roman province of Judea and, as such, he was a man of power, although the story actually reveals his weakness. He had secured his appointment through the influence of his brother who happened to be a friend of the Emperor, Claudius. But Felix's period of office was a stormy one, with unrest in Palestine (as was common).

And the case of Paul brought him a problem. The apostle had been taken into custody during a disturbance in Jerusalem and was being held at the governor's quarters in Caesarea. The beginning of Acts 24 tells of the arrival of the High Priest and a lawyer to press the case against Paul.

The lawyer began with some flattery and then described Paul as 'A plague, one who stirs up riots among all the Jews throughout the world and is a ringleader of the sect of the Nazarenes' (v. 5). Some versions translate the word for 'plague' as 'trouble-maker', which is interesting and reminiscent of the earlier time when Paul and Silas had come to Thessalonica. As Paul preached the gospel there, some people were converted, but the Jews of the town stirred up a riot. Jason had welcomed Paul and Silas, and he found himself the victim of a mob attack on his house. The protesters 'dragged Jason and some of the brothers before the city authorities, shouting, "These men who have turned the world upside down have come here also, and Jason has received them, and they are all acting against the decrees of Caesar, saying that there is another king, Jesus"' (Acts 17:6–7). Jason was fined and the believers were released. But, if that was trouble, let there be more trouble in our world!

Back in Caesarea, Felix gave Paul permission to speak and Acts gives us a summary of what the apostle said (Acts 24:10–21), before

Felix eventually suspended the proceedings pending the arrival of the tribune who had taken Paul into custody.

And that is as far as Felix got with the case. Perhaps it is as far as he *intended* to get with it. From what is said, it seems likely that he adjourned the case in order to get out of the awkwardness of having to make any decision about it. For two years Paul was kept in custody, before Felix was recalled to Rome by the emperor Nero; it is not known what happened to him after that.

As for Paul, Acts 25 tells of his appearance before the next governor, Festus, and of the eventual exercise of his right of appeal to Rome. Luke then tells of that journey to Rome, and Acts ends with Paul in the capital city without telling us what happened afterwards. Perhaps Luke intended to write a sequel; perhaps he was prevented from completing his work; or perhaps he intended Paul's presence in the great capital city of Rome to be seen as the climax of his story for, if the gospel could be established there, it had truly 'arrived'.

As we consider the kind of doubt seen in Felix, we can discern certain things that were in his favour and certain flaws in his character, before we see his final rejection of the challenge before him.

## Factors in his favour

The first thing that could have been to Felix's advantage is found in the statement that he had 'a rather accurate knowledge of the Way' (Acts 24:22). 'The Way' was one summary description of the Christian faith and way of life, and Felix, having been governor of Judea for several years, had apparently picked up a fair amount of information about Christianity; 'accurate knowledge' seems to imply more than a passing or casual awareness. Felix's wife was

Jewish and that may also help to account for his background knowledge.

That existing knowledge could have been to Felix's advantage.

But it is not enough to know something about Christianity, just as you could know all about the principles of analgesic drugs and how they operate on the nervous system but that knowledge by itself would not relieve your headache. Felix was acquainted with *the Way*, but obviously he was not *on* the way.

Another thing that could have been to Felix's advantage is the fact that he enjoyed a good discussion. He liked to talk.

Acts 24:26 says that during the two years when Paul was in custody, Felix 'sent for him often and conversed with him'. It seems that he liked a discussion and he possibly found in Paul someone who was fascinating to meet up with—and, of course, he was always available. Perhaps if Felix had an afternoon free, with no official duties to perform or riots to quell, he may have thought to himself: '*How can I while away a few hours; let's get that prisoner brought in for a nice chat; what's his name again—Paul.*'

But, of course, if having some prior knowledge of Christianity is not enough, neither is the enjoyment of a good discussion. Paul had a phrase in 2 Timothy 3:7 about certain people who were 'always learning and never able to arrive at a knowledge of the truth'. Obviously, there is nothing wrong with enjoying a good-going discussion and liking to hear other people's points of view, but there comes a time for deciding where you stand.

G. K. Chesterton made the interesting remark about H. G. Wells: 'I think he thought that the object of opening the mind is simply opening the mind. Whereas I am incurably convinced that the object of opening the mind, as of opening the mouth, is to shut it again on something solid.'[4] There are people who pride themselves on having an open mind, but Chesterton reminds us that is all very well, but there is a time when decision is needed. For Felix, the fact of enjoying a good-going discussion was not enough. It never is.

The other thing that could have been in Felix's favour was the opportunity of hearing the gospel from Paul—this dynamic ambassador for Christ who had once been so determined to wipe Christianity off the face of the earth but whose life had been so dramatically revolutionised by his conversion (Acts 9:1–19). Paul was travelling all over that Mediterranean world, proclaiming the unsearchable riches of Christ, seeing people brought from darkness to light and establishing churches in one place after another.

It was a privilege for Felix, if only he had realized it, to have the opportunity of a face-to-face dialogue with this man. And he did enjoy listening to Paul, but he was determined not to allow Paul's message to penetrate his mind or heart.

He had the advantage of at least some prior knowledge of Christianity; he liked a good-going discussion; he was possibly drawn to Paul in some ways; and certainly, privileged to hear the gospel from Paul. Yet none of these things is enough. He never did come through to faith because there were certain barriers in the way of his paying serious attention to a message that would call for changes in his life.

### Flaws in his character

(a) One flaw in Felix's character was greed. Acts 24:26 tells of him dismissing Paul, hoping that 'money would be given him by Paul'.

He had said that he would deal with the case 'when Lysias the tribune comes down' (v. 22), but we read of two years passing—which is a long time to come the sixty miles from Jerusalem!

So much for the famous Roman justice! Felix hoped for a bribe. Does that indicate that Paul had some resources behind him? I do not know, but money talks and a bribe might have bought him his freedom. Roman law prohibited governors from accepting bribes—but it was apparently a law more honoured in the breach than in the observance.

And this was one of the things that kept Felix back from any decision about Paul—and, more fundamentally, about Christ.

Paul himself would write, 'The love of money is a root of all kinds of evils' (1 Timothy 6:10). He would go on, 'It is through this craving that some have wandered away from the faith and pierced themselves with many pangs' and we can be sure that many others have been kept from a true Christian commitment by simple greed.

Clearly the Bible does not say it is wrong to have money or to be rich, but it does say that those who (in J. B. Phillips' translation) 'set their hearts on being wealthy'—those to whom that is the number one thing in life—'expose themselves to temptation. They fall into one of the world's traps, and lay themselves open to all sorts of silly and wicked desires, which are quite capable of utterly ruining and destroying their souls.'[5] It kept Felix from making the decision he probably knew he should have made.

(b) A second character flaw in Felix was the desire for popularity. The last words of Acts 24 are: 'Desiring to do the Jews a favour, Felix left Paul in prison.' He himself was removed from office—but Paul was left in prison, not for any crime, but because Felix wanted to curry favour with the Jewish population. In general, the Jews hated Rome and all that it stood for (subjugation and shame for them) but perhaps Felix could earn a few brownie points in their eyes by keeping this troublemaker in jail. Again, so much for the famous impartial justice of Rome!

But it is a perennial snare. How many people are kept from a true commitment to Christ by the desire for popularity? They think people would regard them as stupid and gullible if they began to take seriously the claims of Christ and began to submit to His Lordship.

It may be in relation to acts of dishonesty: *'well, everybody else just accepts it as the done thing.'* It may concern standing apart from gossip and character assassination. It may be that if they regarded Sunday as the Lord's Day and refuse to participate in certain events on Sunday, that could make them very unpopular. It may be standing for the sanctity of life, opposing liberal abortion and moves toward euthanasia. These are examples of ways in which commitment may lead to unpopularity sometimes, and where the doubt is not so much an intellectual issue as a challenge to take an unpopular stand.

'We live in a day and age where what the church believes is the minority position on most of the ethical questions of the day.' So wrote Douglas Kelly, and he went on:

> Plus, much of what we believe is abhorrent to mainstream culture. What we believe about the uniqueness of Christ is seen as intolerant by most people. What we believe concerning the appropriateness of the sexual relationship only within marriage is seen as prudish and impossible. What we believe Scripture clearly teaches about

homosexuality is seen by our current culture as non-loving and even hateful.

And, after considering such matters, he posed the challenge, 'The real question is whether we are willing to endure the shame that comes when we stand for the truth of God's Word.'[6] Some choose rather to hide behind the mask of doubt.

(c) Another factor that contributed to Felix's discomfort relates to his marriage. Luke does not give the full story but the background is that his wife, Drusilla, had been married to someone else until Felix enticed her away to be his wife—his third. This is another reason why Felix wanted to keep Paul, and Paul's message, at arm's length—why he was willing enough for a nicely theoretical discussion about Christianity, so long as it did not get too personal.

And the whole trouble is that the gospel Paul preached, the real thing, does get personal. Paul cut through the superficial talk to the real issues, and that brings us to the other thing about Felix.

**Things Felix did not want to hear**

The record says, 'He sent for Paul and heard him speak about faith in Christ Jesus. And as he reasoned about righteousness and self-control and the coming judgement, Felix was alarmed and said, "Go away for the present. When I get an opportunity, I will summon you"' (Acts 24:24–25).

Such were his delaying tactics, his avoidance strategy. All of this, he felt, was too near the bone.

Some people might have advised Paul to avoid certain subjects— *better to stick with things he'll probably agree with*. But the subjects Felix did not *want* to hear about were the very things that he *needed* to hear about. And Paul was not one to only say things that he felt may be popular or acceptable or politically correct.

As we have seen, this is an issue that faces Christians increasingly in our secular society. There are certain topics that many would regard as off-limits in polite company. But we have to constantly consider where our values come from.

An interesting insight into the issue comes from a speech made by the civil rights leader, Martin Luther King. He was opposed to American involvement in the 1955–1975 Vietnam war. He told of a press reporter asking him the question:

> Dr King, since you face so many criticisms and since you are going to hurt the budget of your organization, don't you feel that you should kind of change and fall in line with the Administration's policy? Aren't you hurting the civil rights movement, and people who once respected you may lose respect for you because you're involved in this controversial issue in taking a stand against the war?

King wrote about it: 'I had to look with a deep understanding of why he raised the question and with no bitterness in my heart, and say to that man, "I'm sorry, sir, but you don't know me. I'm not a consensus leader. I don't determine what is right and wrong by … taking a Gallup poll of the majority opinion."'

He then went on, 'On some positions cowardice asks the question, is it safe? Expediency asks the question, is it politic? Vanity asks the question, is it popular? But conscience asks the question, is it right?'[7]

This is surely the proper attitude, so long as conscience is informed by the revelation God has given in His Word.

The Bible includes the inspired and inspiring story of a prophet called Micaiah (2 Chronicles 18:1–13). Ahab was king of Israel and he was trying to persuade Jehoshaphat, the king of Judah, to join him in a military alliance. Jehoshaphat spoke the cautionary word, 'Inquire first for the word of the Lord' (v. 4).

Many prophets were assembled who unanimously said they should go ahead with their military campaign, but Jehoshaphat was unconvinced. He asked, 'Is there not here another prophet of the Lord of whom we may inquire?' Ahab referred to Micaiah, but said, 'I hate him, for he never prophesies good concerning me, but always evil' (vv. 6–7).

But a messenger was sent to summon Micaiah, and *en route* the messenger advised Micaiah to be politic with his counsel; 'Behold, the words of the prophets with one accord are favourable to the king. Let your word be like the word of one of them, and speak favourably.' Micaiah's answer, however, was, 'As the Lord lives, what my God says, that I will speak' (vv. 12–13).

Felix too wanted to hear what he wanted to hear. And Paul's attitude was to ask, not 'is it safe?' or 'is it politic?' or 'is it popular?'; rather, he would stand by the things that God has revealed. He would not just say what he knew would go down well. He reasoned, we are told, about three things which Felix did not want to hear: righteousness, self-control and the coming judgement.

It is interesting that Acts 24:25 follows on immediately after verse 24! In verse 24, Felix heard Paul 'speak about faith in Christ Jesus', and then the narrative immediately goes on: 'And as he reasoned about righteousness ... Felix was alarmed.' It sounds as if he was happy enough to listen to Paul talking about faith, but when he came to the implications of that 'faith in Christ Jesus', it was then that Felix grew hot under the collar.

Many people are happy with a bit of religious talk and may agree about belief in 'the Man above' or some such vague phrase, but *Jesus as Lord* is another matter. However, so far as the Bible is concerned, we cannot partition Jesus out and accept him as Saviour but not as Lord. Jesus is One, and He is both Saviour and Lord—the One who saves His people from sin and hell, and also the One who calls for our surrender and day-by-day discipleship. Interestingly, the New Testament applies the word, *Saviour*, to Jesus about two dozen times, but it refers to him as *Lord* about six hundred times.

Felix was alarmed when Paul spoke about righteousness; that is what kept him in unbelief rather than faith, in rebellion rather than surrender.

Paul also spoke about self-control—even with Drusilla sitting there. She was rightfully the wife of another man.

There, too, is an issue that threatens many people today in this world of 'easy-come-easy-go' relationships. There are so many mixed-up relationships and so little self-control. This is not to say that wrongdoing in these areas is an unforgiveable sin—that ought to be said because the whole gospel message is about forgiveness and new beginnings. But, in Paul's words about self-control, we see another reason why Felix wanted to cut short the conversation.

And the other thing about which Paul spoke was the judgement to come. If there is to be a judgement ahead, where would Felix stand? He clearly would not relish the thought of having to give account to God on high. It was bad enough to have to give an account to Caesar on high, which Felix did have to do when he was recalled to Rome to answer for his mishandling of disturbances in Judea, especially, along with other irregularities. As one Bible Dictionary says, 'Unrest increased during his rule, for (quoting Tacitus) "with savagery and lust he exercised the powers of a king with the disposition of a slave," and he was utterly merciless in crushing opposition.'[8]

The brother who had secured him his appointment in the first place managed to intervene on his behalf, but nothing is known of Felix's later life.

## Under threat

Doubt can be occasioned by many factors, and many people linger between faith and unbelief because of the moral challenge of Christ. Of course, there are many honest sources of doubt, which need to be sympathetically dealt with, but there are some people who use expressions of doubt to cover up their unwillingness to come to terms with the lordship of Christ. They realize that, if they were to come off the fence and decide for Christ, it would involve changes in their lives—and they are not prepared to face that.

But how sad to allow that to keep them from the Christ who loves people and promises His forgiveness and eternal life to those who will open the door and receive Him into their lives as Saviour and Lord.

Felix had advantages: his prior knowledge about Christianity, his enjoyment of a good discussion, and the opportunity of hearing the gospel from none other than the apostle Paul. But the flaws in his character held him back: his greed for money, his desire for popularity, his marriage to Drusilla. 'Righteousness, self-control and the coming judgement' were not subjects he wanted to hear.

Os Guinness wrote about some questions (not all, as we have seen, but some) as being asked '... not so much to find the truth as to call in question. The questions are placed like a series of carefully laid smoke bombs, designed to cover a well-planned line of retreat. Their aim is ... not so much to get to grips with the problem but to get out of the grip of the answer.'[9]

Similarly, another writer has put it this way in the context of the application of Christian values to public and political life. He suggested that people are 'worried that once God gets out of the box there may be some serious questions to face'.[10] This would have been true for Felix as for many people who would rather that 'religion' was kept in a box hermetically sealed off from daily life.

It is a very different attitude from that of the one-time sceptic, C. S. Lewis, who reflected on the idea that faith is a kind of wish-fulfilment:

> In this view, God is a consoling dream for life's losers, a spiritual crutch for the inadequate and needy. Lewis distances himself from any such idea. The existence of God, Lewis insists, was not something he wished to be true; he valued his independence too much for that. 'I had always wanted, above all things, not to be "interfered with".' In effect, Lewis was confronted with something that he did not *wish* to be true but was forced to conceded *was* true.[11]

He did not want Christianity to be true but he recognized that it *is* true and that the challenges need to be faced.

Felix too did not want Christianity to be true, and we have considered some reasons why he allowed doubt to pull him towards unbelief and rejection of Christ rather than to the response Paul had shown to the gospel message.

Paul also did not *want* Christianity to be true. He said later in his defence before king Agrippa, 'I myself was convinced that I ought to do many things in opposing the name of Jesus of Nazareth' (Acts 26:9). But then came his encounter with the living Christ on the road to Damascus, and 'I was not disobedient to the heavenly vision, but declared first to those in Damascus, then in Jerusalem and throughout all the region of Judea, and also to the Gentiles, that they should repent and turn to God, performing deeds in keeping with their repentance' (vv. 19–20).

In Acts 26:24–27, the next governor, Festus, expressed the view that Paul was out of his mind, to which the apostle responded by insisting that he was speaking true and rational words.

On the same occasion the Jewish king, Agrippa, was sarcastically dismissive, ridiculing the idea that Paul might persuade him to be a Christian. Paul said, 'I would to God that not only you but also all who hear me this day might become such as I am—except for these chains' (v. 29).

And Paul would spend his life, as the last verse of Acts (28:31) says, 'proclaiming the kingdom of God and teaching about the Lord Jesus Christ with all boldness'.

This chapter has been concerned with the kind of doubt that is occasioned by moral rather than intellectual issues. Every sympathetic patience should be shown to people who have genuine doubts and difficulties; the Bible says, 'Have mercy on those who doubt' (Jude 22). But sometimes we need to be challenged about the kinds of doubt that are really 'the special pleading of a dishonest heart to escape from the convictions of conscience'.[12] There are times to simply heed the expression found in Isaiah 30:21—'This is the way, walk in it.'

## NOTES

1  Little, Paul E., *How to Give Away your Faith*, (London: IVP British edition 1971), p. 88.

2  Huxley, A., *Ends and Means*, (London: Chatto & Windus, 1937), p. 273. His brother, Julian, said, 'The sense of spiritual relief which comes from rejecting the idea of God as a supernatural being is enormous.' (D'Souza, Dinesh, *What's So Great About Christianity?* p. 266).

3  Smith, Paul, article in *Evangelical Times*, January 2020, p. 18.

4  Chesterton, C. K., *Autobiography*, (New York: Sheed & Ward, 1936), p. 229.

5  Phillips, J. B., *The New Testament in Modern English*, (London: Geoffrey Bles, 1960).

6  Kelly, Douglas, *Creation and Change*, (Tain: Christian Focus, 2017), p. 328.

7  Speech on 6 February 1968 in Washington, D.C. www.aavw.org/special_features/speeches_speech_king04.html (accessed 14/09/23)

8  *Illustrated Bible Dictionary*, Volume 1 (London: IVP, 1980), p. 505.

9  Guinness, Os, *Doubt*, p.190.

10  Wright T., *Surprised by Scripture*, (London: SPCK, 2014), p. 165.

11  McGrath, A., *C. S. Lewis—A Life*, (London: Hodder & Stoughton, 2013), p. 147.

12  Palmer, Benjamin Morgan, *Selected Writings*, p. 190.

# 13 Who? Me?

## DOUBTS ABOUT THE CALLING OF GOD

Another possible source of doubt concerns the question of whether such a Person as the almighty King of the universe could possibly have any interest in us. Do we matter to Him? And does He have a place for us? It is all very well to read about famous Christians like David Livingstone or Corrie ten Boom, but does God have a place for ordinary people like us?

When Hebrews 11 gives examples of people who lived 'by faith', one of the largest sections is devoted to Moses, the Hebrew who was saved from death soon after he was born, who was brought up by Pharaoh's daughter, and who later killed an Egyptian taskmaster and had to flee to Midian. Hebrews says:

> By faith Moses, when he was grown up, refused to be called the son of Pharaoh's daughter, choosing rather to be mistreated with the people of God than to enjoy the fleeting pleasures of sin. He considered the reproach of Christ greater wealth than the treasures of Egypt, for he was looking to the reward. By faith he left Egypt, not being afraid of the anger of the king, for he endured as seeing him who is invisible. By faith he kept the Passover and sprinkled the blood, so that the Destroyer of the firstborn might not touch them (Hebrews 11:24–28).

This summary of Moses' life tells of a man of great faith; the paradoxical phrase, 'seeing him who is invisible', tells of the faith he held in the unseen God who was nonetheless a God who reveals Himself and speaks to His people.

When we read the account of Moses' life in Exodus, we find that this faith was by no means an easy or superficial faith, and the account of his call to be God's man for the hour reveals something of his struggle to accept that call and to trust that God would guide and uphold him through all the trials and struggles that lay ahead.

He was tending the flock of his father-in-law Jethro, when 'the angel of the LORD appeared to him in a flame of fire out of the midst of a bush. He looked, and behold, the bush was burning.' Some Presbyterians could say the next part in Latin (because the words are written round the image of the burning bush in the logo of many Presbyterian churches—and everything sounds better in Latin!): '*nec tamen consumebatur*; yet it was not consumed' (Exodus 3:1–2).

Then came the call to undertake a task that must have seemed completely absurd. Moses did not doubt God's existence but he did doubt the seriousness of God's call. The voice from the burning bush was telling him that he, a man who was living out a quiet life as a shepherd in Midian and who was there because he had killed a man in Egypt, was to go to the king of the most powerful nation in the world and demand the release of the Hebrew slaves.

If Moses had been of a sarcastic disposition, he might have said, '*Oh is that all!*', followed by, '*Lord, you can't be serious.*' But God *was* serious—and eventually Moses would indeed do it.

Firstly, he heard the voice of the Lord saying, 'I have surely seen the affliction of my people who are in Egypt and have heard their cry because of their taskmasters. I know their sufferings, and I have come down to deliver them' (Exodus 3:7–8). So far so good! Some people might have thought, '*It's about time you took notice*', and now at last God was going to do something about it.

Then, in verse 10, comes the thunderbolt which must have shaken Moses from the top of his head to the sole of his sandals: 'Come, I will send you to Pharaoh that you may bring my people, the children of Israel, out of Egypt.' Suddenly the whole situation looked different. It is one thing to applaud God's intentions in a general way, but this was different; this involved him.

The narrative tells of Moses' struggles which ran the full gamut from self-doubt to doubt about God's power. Future generations would remember him as a great deliverer, an inspiring leader, a fine administrator and lawgiver (all under God), but Moses had his doubts.

And his story is an encouragement for any of us who have doubts about whether God could have a place and a calling for us.

There is an old hymn that speaks of 'a task the Master just for you has planned',[1] but no wonder Moses struggled with this calling. The hymn talks about God having a distinct calling for each of His people. As a student I remember saying to my mentor that I would love to be able to preach like X (a powerful preacher of the time) and receiving the reply that God would rather have five minutes of me preaching as me than thirty-five of me imitating X! We all have a particular calling and even if we feel we cannot do what Mary Slessor or Billy Graham or William Wilberforce did—or Moses—God has His purposes, calling and opportunities for each of us.

Exodus 3 tells of Moses' initial doubts. Some of his responses may seem like excuses but, if they are such, they are based on doubt about the seriousness of God's plan.

Exodus tells of at least four ways in which his doubt is expressed, and they may correspond to some of our doubts.

## 'I'm not gifted enough'

Moses' response to God's call started with him asking the wrong question. He asked, 'Who am I?' instead of, 'Who are You?' He would eventually come to 'Who are You?', but he started with questions about his own inability: 'Who am I that I should go to Pharaoh and bring the children of Israel out of Egypt?' (v. 11).

Pharaoh was one of the most powerful men in the world at that time, and Moses was ...—well, he was *not* one of the most powerful men in the world at that time. So, there is a naturalness about his diffidence. Self-doubt is fair enough up to a point, as we see if we think of its opposite. There would be something suspect about the idea of someone called by God to some difficult task and immediately saying, '*OK, no bother*'!

The point was made by C. S. Lewis in one episode of the Narnia tales:

> Then Peter, leading Caspian, forced his way through the crowd of animals.
> 'This is Caspian, Sir', he said.
> And Caspian knelt and kissed the Lion's paw.
> 'Welcome, Prince,' said Aslan. 'Do you feel yourself sufficient to take up the kingship of Narnia?'
> 'I—I don't think so, Sir,' said Caspian, 'I'm only a kid'.
> 'Good', said Aslan, 'If you had felt yourself sufficient, it would have been a proof that you were not'.[2]

It is a good thing to have a realistic view of one's own limitations. But it is also a great thing to learn (as Moses learned through this whole experience) that if God calls a person to a task, He also equips;

as is sometimes said, 'He doesn't call the equipped but He equips the called.'

This is His answer to Moses' doubt. He says, 'But I will be with you' (verse 12), and if it is a good thing to be humble about ourselves and our own abilities, it is an even greater thing to learn to trust in the God who equips His people for service, so that things otherwise impossible become divinely possible.

With this matter of rescuing the Hebrew slaves from Egypt, it must have seemed crazy to even contemplate it, but it happened.

Similarly, the idea of twelve ordinary men setting out in Jesus' name to change the world also looked impossible, but it happened.

And it is the words, 'But I will be with you' that make all the difference. This is God's answer to Moses' doubts.

In the journal of the medical missionary and explorer, David Livingstone, there is a famous entry. Almost at the end, alone in the heart of Africa, he wrote in shaky handwriting about the promise of Jesus in Matthew 28:20: '"Lo, I am with you aye": It is the word of a gentleman of the most sacred and strict honour and there's an end of it.'[3] That, he said, was what had sustained him through the years.

It is also what changed everything for Moses. It is the answer also to our doubts about whether God's call to discipleship applies to us. It does—and the thing that makes all the difference is this: 'But I will be with you.'

## I don't know enough

If we doubt whether we know enough about God and the Bible to be useful to Him, it may help to know that similar self-doubt was part of Moses' response to God's call. He did not know all the answers: 'If

I come to the people of Israel and say to them, "The God of your fathers has sent me to you", and they ask me, "What is his name?" what shall I say to them?' (Exodus 3:13).

Moses was not the last person to feel such uncertainty and diffidence. Many of us, when confronted by encouragements to witness for Christ and share our faith, feel that we do not know enough to be able to do it; we are afraid of being asked questions which we will not be able to answer.

So, one response is to retreat into an 'actions-speak-louder-than-words' attitude, trusting that the silent witness of life and character will have an influence. Titus 2:10 talks about living lives that 'adorn the doctrine of God our Saviour'.

But, ultimately, words are necessary; there needs to be some kind of verbal testimony to the reality of God and the truth of the gospel. And believers need to seek, so far as they can, to be able to give a reasoned account of the gospel (1 Peter 3:15), doing so with gentleness and respect. This will involve studying the Scriptures, thinking about the application of the gospel to today's world and considering the objections people make to belief.

But in the last analysis, there is no shame in uttering the simple phrase, '*I don't know.*' We will not be able to answer all the possible questions that may be thrown up and there comes a time when the only thing to do is to say, '*I don't know the answer to that question.*' It may be possible to say you will try to find more information, but faithful witness does not depend on being able to give full answers to every question.

Think of the formerly blind man of John chapter 9. All sorts of questions were being raised by Jesus' enemies. One of their attacks was the idea that Jesus was 'a sinner' and the now-sighted man replied, 'Whether he is a sinner I do not know. One thing I do know, that though I was blind, now I see' (vv. 24–25). They may badger him till the cows come home (to mix metaphors furiously!) but they could not deny that something had happened.

In a similar vein, it is possible to give a list of arguments for the historicity of Christ's physical resurrection from the dead, but it has been written of the early Christians:

> The evidence they offered was neither signed statements of neutral observers nor closely reasoned philosophic arguments: it was the evidence of lives changed utterly by contact with the risen Christ. And today, if anything will shake and persuade the mocker, perhaps it will not be our arguments; it will be the degree of our own conviction. And that depends always upon the reality of our own personal commitment to the risen Lord.[4]

If Moses' doubt represents the feeling that, even if we have been Christians for a long time, we do not really know enough and there are still questions that baffle us, then we can be encouraged that even this great leader and prophet felt that way. But his effectiveness did not depend on knowing all the answers to all the questions that can be posed.

However far we have come along the road of Christian discipleship, there is so much more to learn from God's own self-revelation, and even though we do not know everything, we do know something. We know our own story and testimony. We could even put the point this way: if we were to wait until we understood everything about God and His Word, we would never do anything. If

Moses had waited until he knew all the answers to all the questions, the Hebrews might still be in Egyptian captivity!

However, what we do find in the burning bush story is that, when he moved from asking, 'Who am I to undertake this task?' to 'Who are You?' he was given the enigmatic answer: '"I AM WHO I AM". And he said, "Say this to the people of Israel, 'I AM has sent me to you'"' (Exodus 3:14).

He is the God who exists; He is, in the title of one of Francis Schaeffer's books, 'The God who is there.'[5] He is not a figment of human imagination; he is not a Santa Claus figure that people have invented to amuse themselves; he is not a projection on to a higher plane of some human needs. He is the God who exists—always has done and always will—the God who has always been there, who is now and who will be there for ever. He is the eternally self-existent One, with no beginning or end, the great I AM.

He is also the God who reveals Himself in His actions and, in response to Moses' doubts, He reminds Moses that He is 'The LORD, the God of your fathers, the God of Abraham, the God of Isaac, and the God of Jacob' (v. 15). He is the God who had led Abraham and promised him a land and a people; the One who fulfilled the impossible promise of a child for Sarah in her old age; the God who blessed Isaac; the God who acted in the life of even a rascal like Jacob and turned him into *Israel*, the father of the nation. This is the God, Moses was to say, who has sent me to rescue you from slavery.

For us, it goes further. We have the whole record of God's mighty deeds through the succeeding centuries, centring of course in the coming life, death and resurrection of Jesus. We have less reason than Moses for saying that we do not know enough about God—we who have the words of John 1:18: 'No one has ever seen God; the only God, who is at the Father's side, he has made him known.'

John refers in these words to God the Father and then to God the Son and says that the Son has 'made him known' (literally, *exegeted him, drawn him out*). 'In him', Paul writes, 'all the fulness of God was pleased to dwell' (Colossians 1:19).

All-in-all, we have a fuller answer to the question Moses asked about who God is and, although we may still have unanswered questions, God has given us more light: through the study of the Scriptures we can be reproved, corrected, trained and equipped for every good work (2 Timothy 3:16).

### People will not believe me

Another source of doubt is the assumption that people will not believe us or even pay attention to what we say. This was the third doubt expressed by Moses about God's call on his life. Exodus 4:1: 'Moses answered, "But behold, they will not believe me or listen to my voice, for they will say, 'The LORD did not appear to you.'"'

It was another reason for Moses to doubt the reality or seriousness of God's call—*nobody will pay any attention to me; they won't believe that God has called me.*

In answer, God gave Moses three special miraculous signs: his rod turned into a snake; his hand turned leprous and back again; and water turned to blood. These would be astounding signs that would bear witness to the fact that God was working through him—signs that would answer his own doubts about whether people would listen to him.

We live now in a time when it is very tempting to retreat behind *'they'll never believe me'*. There are some who violently oppose Christianity but there are many others who just assume that it is an old story—something that people once believed but not any longer.

Such a shell of bland assumption is not easy to crack and, generally, we do not now have miraculous actions to validate our claims. Moses' story comes from one of the particular periods of miracles in God's purposes. Many miracles happened around this time of the Exodus; then again in the times of Elijah and Elisha; and of course, around the earthly ministry of Jesus. Many people assume that the Bible is a miracle-a-page book, but it is not so, and it has been estimated that if you average it out there may be evidence for one miracle about every thirty years; many ordinary people could have lived their whole life without ever witnessing an event that was out of the ordinary.[6]

For people who reject the whole notion of miracles, the redoubtable G. K. Chesterton provided a vigorous response:

> My belief that miracles have happened in human history is not a mystical belief at all; I believe in them upon human evidences as I do in the discovery of America. Upon this point there is a simple logical fact that only requires to be stated and cleared up. Somehow or other an extraordinary idea has arisen that disbelievers in miracles consider them coldly and fairly, while believers in miracles accept them only in connection with some dogma. The fact is quite the other way. The believers in miracles accept them (rightly or wrongly) because they have evidence for them. The disbelievers in miracles deny them (rightly or wrongly) because they have a doctrine against them.[7]

Similarly, Professor John Lennox has written, 'The rejection of the supernatural in principle is unscientific—and indeed irrational.'[8]

But, for the present, it is not generally through such miraculous signs as were given to Moses that God works. And perhaps for now the answer to '*people won't believe us*' is the evidence of changed lives—which is, in a different way, a miracle also. We need a contemporary form of the description which Michael Green has given of the testimony of the early Christians: 'They made the grace of God credible by a society of love and mutual care which astonished the pagans and was recognized as something entirely new. It lent persuasiveness to their claim that the new age had dawned in Christ.'[9] Making the grace of God credible is the calling of the church, and its challenge. If we feel as Moses felt—*they won't listen*—it is for us to make the gospel credible in the eyes of the world by the lives we live, the testimony we maintain and the love we show.

## You cannot mean me!

Moses entertained doubts about his own giftedness, his knowledge of God and the improbability of being believed. His other doubt was about whether God could really be serious in calling *him*.

'Oh, my Lord, I am not eloquent, either in the past or since you have spoken to your servant, but I am slow of speech and of tongue' (Exodus 4:10), and when God said He would teach Moses what to say, he finally came out with, 'Oh, my Lord, please send someone else!' (4:13).

As to his assertion that he was not eloquent, we find an interesting description of Moses in Acts 7:22 as 'mighty in his words and deeds' (the New English Bible translates it, 'a powerful speaker and a man of action'), and as to the second, God would send Aaron with Moses to help with the speaking. These were the ways in which God answered this expression of doubt from Moses.

If we, in our very different circumstances, are inclined to the same doubts as Moses had, we can learn from the responses Moses received. The instruction for Jesus' followers, 'You will be my witnesses' is preceded by the promise, 'You will receive power when the Holy Spirit has come upon you' (Acts 1:8). We are not left alone, because we work in fellowship with other believers in mutual encouragement, and also because we are assured of the help and guidance of the Holy Spirit as we seek to witness for Him.

If we are tempted to think there are others better equipped than we are, we should remember these promises of the Lord and realize that there are opportunities open to us that may not be open to anyone else.

Even Moses—great leader, deliverer, prophet and law-giver—had doubts: doubts about his own suitability, his knowledge of God, how people would respond to him and whether God could really be calling *him*. God's responses can encourage us if we have similar doubts about our suitability for service.

### NOTES

1  Hymn, 'There's a work for Jesus', by Elsie D. Yale, 1873–1956.
2  Lewis, C. S., *Prince Caspian* in illustrated *Complete Chronicles of Narnia*, (Glasgow: Collins, 1998, original written in 1951), p. 280.
3  www.wholesomewords.org/missions/bliving8.html (accessed 14/09/23)
4  Stewart, James S., *A Faith to Proclaim*, (London: Hodder & Stoughton, 1953), p. 116.
5  Schaeffer, Francis, *The God who is there*, (Westmont, Illinois: InterVarsity Press, 1998).
6  Goldsworthy, Graham, *Preaching the Whole Bible as Christian Scripture*, (London: IVP, 2000), p. 196.

7   Chesterton, C. K., *Orthodoxy*, (Dover Publications edition of 2004; originally published by Dodd, Mead & Company in 1908), p. 143.

8   Lennox, Prof. John, *Against the Flow*, (Oxford: Monarch Books, 2015), p. 215.

9   Green, Michael, *Evangelism in the Early Church*, (London: Hodder & Stoughton, 1970), p. 120.

# 14 After the mountain top

## DOUBTS ABOUT THE CAUSE OF GOD

'Take my life and let it be consecrated, Lord, to thee,' is the opening phrase of a well-known hymn.[1] It expresses the desire for every part of life to be consecrated to the living God.

When the words appear in 1 Kings 19:4, however, they have a rather different thrust. The prophet Elijah was mired in depression and doubt, and his prayer was that God would end his life: 'He sat down under a broom tree. And he asked that he might die, saying, "It is enough; now, O LORD, take away my life."'

True, it is *to God* that he addresses this request, which shows that he has not lost faith in a God who hears the prayers of His people, and he is not suicidal because he places his life in God's hands, but he is depressed and tempted to doubt the purposes and power of the Lord whom he has sought to serve.

So, great prophet as he was, Elijah's faith crisis may be helpful to others who pass through such a dark tunnel.

It may be doubt about the reality of our own experience. Perhaps there was a time of great blessing, a 'mountain-top experience', but later we wondered whether it was all real. It seemed real at the time: there was a real uplift, perhaps through participation in some great service or convention; perhaps at a time of public profession of faith when everything seemed very real; or perhaps even in a literal 'mountain-top experience' when we were captivated by the beauty of God's creation.

Such high moments can come in various ways, but so can the experience we sometimes describe as 'coming back down to earth'. It may bring the temptation to wonder: *was it all real, or did I just get carried away?*

It may be doubt about the effectiveness of our example and witness. The word of Christ is, 'You will receive power when the Holy Spirit has come upon you, and you will be my witnesses' (Acts 1:8), and we may also recall Peter's words about being always ready to give a reason for the hope we have (1 Peter 3:15). We also know Jesus' word: 'By this all people will know that you are my disciples, if you have love for one another' (John 13:35). However, it is possible to become so aware of our inadequacies and failures in these areas that we can doubt whether God could really have any time for us.

Or it may be doubt about the future of the cause of Christ. We believe in Him; we read the ringing words of Revelation 11:15 about a time when it will be said that 'The kingdom of the world has become the kingdom of our Lord and of his Christ, and he shall reign for ever and ever.' Yet, at the same time, we recognize that western society is becoming increasingly secularized.

We see redundant church buildings, we hear of ageing congregations, and we know that many people assume that, while the sea of faith was once at full tide, now we can 'only hear its melancholy, long, withdrawing roar, retreating ... down the ... naked shingles of the world'.[2]

I noticed some months ago that, whereas BBC Television once used to broadcast a Sunday morning service, they were advertising a programme entitled, 'The Way We Worshipped'; the implication seems to be that religion is part of our past, a thing we look back on—perhaps even with fondness—but a thing of the past.

There are many factors in our world today (not in the wider world, of course, but in western society) that might make us fearful about the future of God's work. We know it is silly—and unscriptural—to think that way, and yet ...

Well, Elijah faced such temptations to doubt. If we were reading the Bible for the first time and we had read the story of 1 Kings 18, we would expect chapter 19 to be headed with something like, 'To God be the glory; great things He has done,'[3] or, if you were in the Scouts, 'Riding along on the crest of the wave'. That is where Elijah should have been, because chapter 18 told the momentous story of the confrontation on Mount Carmel.

King Ahab and Queen Jezebel were introducing Baal worship into Israel. Elijah resisted their efforts and things came to a head at Carmel. Hundreds of people gathered there, including the '450 prophets of Baal and the 400 prophets of Asherah' (1 Kings 18:19); it says they ate at Jezebel's table, which signifies more than their food supplies. It means that they were aided and abetted by Jezebel ('By Appointment', you might say).

On the other side was Elijah: one man who was determined that Baalism should not rule; one man who would stand up for the Lord, however lonely a stand that was.

His challenge to the people was: 'How long will you go limping between two different opinions? If the LORD is God, follow him; but if Baal, then follow him' (v. 21).

And the story tells of the 'contest' as the prophets of Baal called on their gods to send fire to consume their offering: 'But there was no voice, and no one answered' (v. 26).

Then Elijah called on the Lord to send fire and, in verse 38, 'The fire of the LORD fell and consumed the burnt offering and the wood and the stones and the dust, and licked up the water that was in the trench' (to prevent any allegation of trickery).

It was a huge vindication for Elijah—a victory for the Lord, of course, but a massive vindication of Elijah as the Lord's servant.

So, chapter 19, as we have suggested, ought to be a chapter of great rejoicing, but instead we find Elijah in gloom and despondency and in terror of the wrath of Jezebel. The queen had been shown up in public and she was out for Elijah's blood. And we find Elijah sitting under a tree, praying that God would just end his life there and then.

Just as we may sometimes doubt the effectiveness of our witness, Elijah wondered what impact he was making. When he says in 1 Kings 19:4, 'I am no better than my fathers,' presumably he means: *no better at turning people to God than others who went before me.*

In verse 14 he says, 'I have been very jealous for the LORD, the God of hosts. For the people of Israel have forsaken your covenant, thrown down your altars, and killed your prophets with the sword.' This is how Elijah felt—had it all been useless? All his zeal and enthusiasm and fearless witness had not turned people to the living God.

Elijah was fearful for the future of God's cause. Jezebel had made her vow that within twenty-four hours Elijah would be dead and, since he had been seen at Carmel as, very publicly, the prophet of the Lord, that would signal the victory of Jezebel and her Baalism over the God of Elijah and of Israel.

The narrative continues Elijah's lament, 'The people of Israel have forsaken your covenant, thrown down your altars, and killed your prophets with the sword, and I, even I only, am left, and they seek my life, to take it away' (v. 14).

In different ways, people today may fear for the cause of the Lord. In western society, it seems that the church is not the force that it once was and evangelism is increasingly difficult in a society where people do not want to know what we proclaim, much less see it as good news. In theory we believe that history is His story, that 'Jesus shall reign,'[4] and that even the gates of hell shall not prevail against the true church of the living God (Matthew 16:18), but there are times when doubts creep in.

In that sense we can sympathize with Elijah in his time of depression and doubt. Twice in 1 Kings 19 we find him faced with the question, 'What are you doing here?' (vv. 9 and 13). He was hiding in a cave but the question may be taken as referring not simply to his physical whereabouts (*why are you hiding in this cave?*) but to his inner condition of depression and doubt—*what are you doing in this frame of heart and mind?*

The Scottish athlete, Eric Liddell, is famous for his refusal to compete on a Sunday, even in the Olympic Games and even when he was accused of being unpatriotic and arrogant. The story is well-known of his remarkable victory instead in an event for which he had not trained. Not so well known is the story of another athletic meeting at which he was competing, when he was jostled by a fellow runner so that he lay sprawled out beside the track. Many would have been tempted to give up but someone yelled, 'Get up and run', and Liddell did get up and proceeded to win the race in what the *Scotsman* newspaper called 'a performance bordering on the miraculous'.[5]

Here we see Elijah knocked off course. What was it that tripped him up? As well as the main spiritual issue behind his doubts, we may notice certain very human factors which caused him to stumble; fear, exhaustion, loneliness and discouragement played a part in his predicament.

## Fear

We are told plainly, 'He was afraid, and he arose and ran for his life' (1 Kings 19:3), first to Beersheba and then a further day's journey into the wilderness. This man who had stood fearlessly at Mount Carmel and faced the 450 prophets of Baal and 400 prophets of Asherah, was now afraid of the wrath of one woman! According to a well-known saying, 'hell hath no fury like a woman scorned,'[6] and here is this powerful woman (perhaps all the more powerful because her husband was weak) breathing out threats of slaughter against this disciple of the Lord.

Elijah was no coward, but he was afraid.

The Bible says, 'Trust in the Lord with all your heart, and do not lean on your own understanding. In all your ways acknowledge him, and he will make straight your paths' (Proverbs 3:5–6); it says, 'Do not be frightened, and do not be dismayed, for the Lord your God is with you wherever you go' (Joshua 1:9); it says, 'Be strong in the Lord and in the strength of his might' (Ephesians 6:10)—but it is easy to forget such things.

That was true in Elijah's time and it is true in our time also—a time when we are very concerned about the way the social tide is flowing and when Christian people can feel a kind of fear in the face of the enemies of the gospel.

We are in a better position than Elijah in that we now have the whole Bible to teach, inspire and strengthen us. As David Livingstone would testify when receiving an honorary doctorate in Glasgow in 1856, with his left arm hanging by his side as the result of an encounter with a lion, 'Would you like me to tell you what supported me through all the years of exile among a people whose language I could not understand and whose attitude toward me was always uncertain and often hostile?' He answered his own question: 'It was this—"Lo, I am with you always, even to the end of the world" (Matthew 28:20, AKJV). On these words I staked everything and they never failed.'[7]

The writer to the Hebrews echoed that verse: '… he has said, "I will never leave you nor forsake you." So, we can confidently say, "The Lord is my helper; I will not fear; what can man do to me?"' (Hebrews 13:5–6, quoting Psalm 118:6).

There are many words of promise which encourage us, even in down times, to look up and know that if He is for us, nothing can ultimately be against us (Romans 8:31).

## Exhaustion

After the drama of Mount Carmel, Elijah was physically and mentally exhausted and it might not sound very spiritual to say, '*Elijah, you need a rest*', but that was the truth. Elijah needed rest and food, and God saw to it that he got both. He was sleeping and when he awoke 'there was at his head a cake baked on hot stones and a jar of water. And he ate and drank and lay down again' (1 King 19:6).

It happened again and he was enabled to go 'in the strength of that food forty days and forty nights to Horeb, the mount of God' (v. 8)—the place where God had spoken to Moses and where He would now speak to Elijah.

This was part of God's remedy for Elijah's breakdown—he needed rest and food. God is the God of the everyday and even the humdrum as much as He is the God of the high moments.

Sometimes this is not easy medicine to take—we think God should do something spectacular, even miraculous, and certainly more significant than saying, '*Get to bed earlier and consider your diet*.' But God has made us in such a way that we cannot simply ignore such matters and expect to stay fit, either physically or spiritually.

## Loneliness

Elijah's explanation of his depression was, 'The people of Israel have forsaken your covenant, thrown down your altars, and killed your prophets with the sword, and I, even I only, am left, and they seek my life, to take it away' (verse 10). He felt as if everyone else was going another way and he was the only one who was seeking to honour the living God.

And how did God answer him? 1 Kings 19:18—'Yet I will leave seven thousand in Israel, all the knees that have not bowed to Baal, and every mouth that has not kissed him.' There was a faithful remnant. Perhaps seven thousand is a round number but the point is that Elijah was *not* the only one left. There was for him the reassurance that others too would remain faithful to the Lord.

It does us all good to remember that we are not the only ones who seek to trust and honour Him. All over the world the Spirit is moving and in many places the gospel is spreading like wildfire.

The assurance that comes to us through Elijah's story is that the Lord's cause will prevail long after we are gone from this earthly scene; we are to trust in His eternal purposes.

Of course, there is the call to remain faithful even if we *are* the only ones in our particular situation of family or friends or our workplace. We are to dare to stand alone like Daniel, but there is also great reassurance and strength in the knowledge that God has His people. Crowns and thrones may perish, kingdoms rise and wane—that is the story of history—but the church of Jesus constant will remain—not because we have superior ability or resources, but because we have Christ's own promise and that cannot fail.[8]

## Discouragement

An old fable tells of the devil going out of business (if only!) and selling his tools to anyone who would pay up. His tools were set out: malice, hatred, envy, jealousy, sensuality, deceit and so on, but set apart from the others was a simple wedge-shaped tool which was priced higher than any of the others. When asked, the devil explained: 'That's discouragement. It is a more useful tool to me than all the others. With it I can prise open and get into people's consciousness when I can't get near them with any of the others. And when once inside, I can use the tool in any way that suits me.' He said it was worn because he used it with many people, and the story says it was never sold because the price was too high. He still uses it.

We should not credit the devil with too much power—he does not really own anything—but it is true that the Bible has much to say about his nefarious activities. It says, 'Your adversary the devil prowls around like a roaring lion, seeking someone to devour' (1 Peter 5:8).

And he made good use of the tool in the case of Elijah. Perhaps the prophet had thought that the great victory of Carmel would signal a mighty reversal or renewal or revival. The physical factors mentioned played their part; so did discouragement as it seemed as if the Lord's cause was being thwarted.

When Elijah responded to the Lord's calling by saying, 'I have been very jealous for the LORD, the God of hosts … and I, even I only, am left,' perhaps the emphasis should be on the personal pronouns; '*I* have been zealous for *you*', as if he might add, '*So what about it, Lord? Isn't it time for you to be zealous for me?*'

## Spiritual dryness

Elijah then was afraid; he was exhausted; and he was lonely. His deeper problem, however, was a spiritual one. So long as he kept his eye on the Lord and His purposes, he was strong, but when he allowed Jezebel's threats to loom larger than God's promises, he lost ground.

Even after Carmel and that mighty display of God's power—and of Elijah's spiritual strength and moral courage—he took his eye off the Lord and saw Jezebel. This is often behind *our* times of depression and doubt.

Elijah's great need was to get back his focus on the Lord and His mighty power, and if there is a 'Jezebel' that looms larger in our minds than the living Lord, we need a greater concentration on the Lord Himself.

Elijah travelled on to Sinai. There 'the Lord of might who' ... 'in ancient times gave the law in cloud and majesty and awe'[9] would now speak to Elijah—only, not in the loudness of thunder and lightning but in 'a still small voice'—to use the familiar AKJV form of the ESV's 'sound of a low whisper' (1 Kings 19:12).

The question of verse 9 is repeated in verse 13: 'What are you doing here, Elijah?'—not so much *here at Horeb* as '*here in this state of doubt and depression? Why are you running away from Jezebel and why are you praying that I would take away your life and why are you moaning about being the only believer left in the world?*'

Of course, Elijah had to face the realities of his situation—Jezebel *was* after his blood. The way of faith is not about denying the problems of life or hiding from reality; it is rather about faith in One who is mightier than the noise of many waters (Psalm 93:4) and who is 'able to do far more abundantly than all that we ask or think, according to the power at work within us' (Ephesians 3:20).

We need to learn to listen, to hear that still small voice, to pray with the hymn-writer:

> Drop Thy still dews of quietness,
> Till all our strivings cease;
> Take from our souls the strain and stress
> And let our ordered lives confess
> The beauty of Thy peace.
>
> Breathe through the heats of our desire
> Thy coolness and Thy balm;

Let sense be dumb, let flesh retire;
Speak through the earthquake wind and fire,
O still, small voice of calm.[10]

I remember hearing about two Americans walking along a busy street in New York City. One was a native American and, amid all the hustle and bustle of the noisy street, he said, 'Listen, I can hear a cricket.' His companion was sceptical; how could he possibly hear a cricket amid all the noise around them? But his friend insisted and eventually tracked the sound to a waste bucket into which he delved until, at last, he came out with the cricket in his hand.

His friend was amazed; he said, 'You must have the most amazing ears.' But the other responded, 'No, I don't have amazing ears. I have ears just like everyone else's, but my ears are attuned to hear that kind of sound. Everything depends on what your ears are attuned to.'

To illustrate his point, he took out a handful of loose coins and threw them up into the air. When they landed on the pavement (or sidewalk, since we are in New York), even though the traffic noise was loud, people for several blocks stopped and looked around. They recognized *that* sound; their ears were attuned to the sound of money!

The Bible says, 'He who has ears to hear, let him hear' (e. g., Matthew 11:15; Mark 4:9; Luke 14:35).

If we have similar experiences to Elijah's—times when we wonder whether some great experience was real, or whether our witness has made any difference, or when we fear for the future of God's cause—we can learn from the prophet's experience of fear, exhaustion and loneliness, and from his renewed hearing of the Word of the living God.

If he had been a New Testament believer, he might be described as one who got back on track to 'run with endurance the race that is set before him, looking to Jesus, the founder and perfecter of our faith, who for the joy that was set before him endured the cross, despising the shame, and is seated at the right hand of the throne of God' (Hebrews 12:1–2).

In 1 Kings 19:15, Elijah was told to go back—back to the hard realities of the situation that faced him, but with renewed confidence and renewed courage. The message was: '*Elijah, you can't run away from the world and all its problems and difficulties; you can't remain in this self-pity and doubt—there is a job to be done.*'

In our case it may translate as this: '*Go back to your home, your place of work, your school or university, your circle of friends where it may not be easy to live a consistent Christian life, but go back, remembering God's remedy for such doubts: look after your health, remember you are part of a great fellowship of faith, listen to God's still small voice.*'

In times of spiritual dryness, the worst thing to do is to ignore the Bible, neglect prayer and give up going to church or any Christian group of which we are a part.

**NOTES**

1   Havergal, Frances R., 'Take my life and let it be consecrated, Lord, to Thee', 1836–1879.

2   Lines from poem, 'Dover Beach', by Matthew Arnold, 1822–88. Rintoul, F. and Skinner, J. B., *Poet's Quair*, (Edinburgh & London: Oliver & Boyd, 1950), p. 362.

3   Hymn written by Fanny Crosby, 1820–1915.

4   Hymn, based on Psalm 72, by Isaac Watts, 1674–1748.

5   Quoted in: Hamilton, Duncan, *For The Glory*, (London: Transworld Publishers, 2016), p. 78.

6　From *The Mourning Bride*, a play written by William Congreve in 1697.

7　Matthews, Basil, *Livingstone, the Pathfinder*, (London: Livingstone Press, 1948), pp. 83–84.

8　From the hymn, 'Onward, Christian soldiers', by Sabine Baring-Gould, 1834–1924.

9　From the hymn, 'O come, O come, Emmanuel', twelfth-century Latin hymn translated by John Mason Neale, 1818–66.

10　From the hymn, 'Dear Lord and Father of mankind', by John Greenleaf Whittier, 1807–92.

# Epilogue

One danger of a book like this is that it pays too much attention to doubt, which has been likened to attention-seeking children—the more attention they get, the more they demand.

In actual fact, although we have been considering doubts and doubters, this book is more about faith than doubt. If we consider the maxim, 'Feed your faith and your doubts will starve to death', I trust that this has been an encouragement to do just that—to allow God, through His Word, to feed our faith so that the doubts starve to death. 'We must pay much closer attention to what we have heard, lest we drift away from it' (Hebrews 2:1).

\* \* \*

We conclude with an extended quotation from John Bunyan's famous allegory, *The Pilgrim's Progress*.[1]

Christian and Hopeful had come to a point where 'a little before them there was on the left hand of the road, a meadow, and a stile to go over into it, and that meadow is called By-Path Meadow.' There Giant Despair captured them and 'drove them before him and put them into his castle, into a very dark dungeon, nasty and stinking to the spirit of these two men.'

A few days later:

> Now when night was come and when Mrs Diffidence, and her
> husband, the Giant, were gone to bed, they began to renew their

discourse of their prisoners: and withal, the old Giant wondered that he could neither by his blows nor counsel bring them to an end. And with that his wife replied, 'I fear,' said she, 'that they live in hope that some will come to relieve them, or that they have pick-locks about them; by the means of which they hope to escape.' 'And, sayest thou so, my dear,' said the Giant, 'I will therefore search them in the morning.'

Well, on Saturday about midnight they began to pray, and continued in prayer till almost break of day.

Now a little before it was day, good Christian, as one half amazed, brake out in this passionate speech, 'What a fool,' quoth he, 'am I, thus to lie in a stinking dungeon, when I may as well walk at liberty. I have a key in my bosom, called promise, that will (I am persuaded) open any lock in Doubting-Castle.'

Then said Hopeful, 'That's good news; good brother, pluck it out of thy bosom, and try.' Then Christian pulled it out of his bosom, and began to try at the dungeon door, whose bolt (as he turned the key) gave back, and the door flew open with ease, and Christian and Hopeful both came out.

Then he went to the outward door that leads into the castle-yard, and with his key opened the door also... Then they went on, and came to the King's highway again, and so were safe, because they were out of his jurisdiction.

Now when they were gone over the stile, they began to contrive with themselves what they should do at that stile to prevent those that should come after from falling into the hands of Giant Despair. So, they consented to erect a pillar, and to engrave upon the side thereof: Over this stile is the way to Doubting-Castle, which is kept by Giant Despair, who despiseth the King of the Celestial Country, and seeks to destroy his holy pilgrims. Many therefore that followed after, read what was written, and escaped the danger. This done, they sang as follows:

Out of the way we went, and then we found
What 'twas to tread upon forbidden ground;
And let them that come after have a care,
Lest heedlessness makes them as we to fare,
Lest they for trespassing his prisoners are,
Whose castle's Doubting, and whose name's Despair.

## NOTES

1 Bunyan, John, *The Pilgrim's Progress*, (Harmondsworth: Penguin Books edition, 1965; originally written in 1678), pp. 149–157.

# Postscript – practical lessons

Distillation of practical points to remember about dealing with doubt:

- The Bible itself includes honest accounts of doubts and doubters.
- God can 'take it' when you bring your doubts to Him.
- You are not the only person who has ever had doubts.
- In times of doubt, your faith is being tested.
- In this life you will never be able to understand or explain everything.
- 'Under the sun' is not the whole of reality.
- We humans are made in God's image (not the other way round).
- Your physical and emotional health can affect your inner disposition.
- Moods and feelings are not reliable guides on issues of truth.
- Do not cut yourself off from the community of faith, even for the meantime.
- The devil wants to undermine your view of God's Word.
- Keep your focus on Jesus and what He said and did.
- Keep praying, even in the dark days.
- Doubt should not be used as a cover for an unwillingness to face the moral challenge of Christ.
- When you know what is right or wrong, do not prevaricate.

- Do not use doubt as an excuse for refusing to take an unpopular stand.
- You are a unique individual who matters to God and He has a calling for you.

# Appendix to chapter 1

With acknowledgements to Mr Charlie Webster of Broughty Ferry, Dundee, who leads regular heritage walks in the burgh.

Back in 1854, Vice-Admiral Robert FitzRoy of the British Royal Navy initiated a programme of placing barometers in fishing communities throughout the British Isles; many are still in place, and they were intended as basic weather forecasters for fishermen. On the morning of 14 October 1881, the fishermen of the fishing community of Broughty Ferry consulted their barometer. Although the sea was calm, the barometric pressure was low; the fishermen decided to trust the barometer and so did not put to sea.

On the same morning, in the town of Eyemouth, the fishermen consulted their barometer but, despite what they saw (and against the advice of some retired fishermen), they decided to put to sea (partly from economic necessity).

Later that day, an unusually severe storm blew up, and the tragic outcome was that 189 Eyemouth fishermen were lost at sea, leaving many widows and more than 200 children were rendered fatherless (the day is still remembered by some as Black Friday).

The tragedy occurred because the Eyemouth men trusted their own instincts rather than their instruments while the men of Broughty Ferry survived because they trusted their instruments rather than their instincts.

The tragic story points to another lesson germane to the theme of this chapter. When doubts and fears arise, we would do well to trust the 'instruments' God has given us rather than trusting our own feelings and instincts. Proverbs 3:5-6 tells us: 'Trust in the LORD with all your heart, and do not lean on your own understanding. In all your ways acknowledge him, and he will make straight your paths.'

# Sources

Aitken, Jonathan, *Pride and Perjury*, (London: Harper Collins, 2000).

Bainton, Roland, *Here I stand: A Life of Martin Luther*, (Nashville: Abingdon Press, 1950 edition).

Bakewell, Joan, *Belief*, (London: Duckworth, 2005).

Bruce, F. F., *In Retrospect*, (Glasgow: Pickering & Inglis, 1980).

Bunyan, John, *The Pilgrim's Progress*, (Harmondsworth: Penguin edition of 1965)

Chapman, Colin, *Christianity On Trial*, (Berkhamsted: Lion, 1971).

Chesterton, C. K., *Autobiography*, (New York: Sheed & Ward, 1936).

Chesterton, C. K., *Orthodoxy*, (Mineola, New York: Dover Publications edition, 2004).

Dallimore, Arnold, *George Whitefield*, (Edinburgh: Banner of Truth, 1980).

Davis, D. R., *The Message of Daniel*, (London: IVP, 2013).

Dawkins, R., *The God Delusion*, (London: Black Swan, 2007).

D'Souza, Dinesh, *What's So Great About Christianity?* (Washington, DC: Regnery Publishing, 2007).

Ferguson, Sinclair B., *Some Pastors And Teachers*, (Edinburgh: Banner of Truth, 2017).

Flew, Antony, *There Is A God*, (New York: HarperCollins, 2007).

Goldsworthy, Graham, *Preaching the Whole Bible as Christian Scripture*, (London: IVP, 2000).

Green, Michael, *Evangelism in the Early Church*, (London: Hodder & Stoughton, 1970).

Green, Michael, *Man Alive!* (London: IVP, 1967).

Griffin, H. W., *The Authentic Voice*, (Tring, Herts: Lion, 1988).

Guinness Os, *Doubt*, (Berkhamsted, Lion Publishing, 1976).

Gunn, G. S., *The Indispensable Christ*, (London: James Clarke, 1962).

Hamilton, Duncan, *For The Glory*, (London: Transworld Publishers, 2016).

Hobbes, Thomas, *Leviathan*, (Everyman edition; originally published 1651).

*Illustrated Bible Dictionary*, Volume 1, (London: IVP, 1980).

Kelly, Douglas, *Creation and Change*, (Tain: Christian Focus, 2017).

Lennox, John, *Against the Flow*, (Oxford: Monarch Books, 2015).

Lewis, C. S., *Complete Chronicles of Narnia*, (Glasgow: Collins, 1998, original written in 1951).

Lewis, C. S., *Mere Christianity*, (London: Collins, 1966; originally published in 1952).

Lewis, C. S., *Miracles*, (London & Glasgow: Collins, 1947).

Lewis, C. S., *Surprised by Joy*, (London: Fontana Books, 1955).

Little, Paul E., *How to Give Away your Faith*, (London: IVP British edition 1971).

McGrath, A., *C. S. Lewis—A Life*, (London: Hodder & Stoughton, 2013).

McGrath, A., *Doubt—Handling it honestly*, (London: IVP, 1990).

McGrath, A., *T. F. Torrance—An Intellectual Biography*, (Edinburgh: T & T Clark, 1999).

McGrath, A., *Why God Won't Go Away*, (London: SPCK, 2011).

McLellan, Alex, *A Jigsaw Guide to Making Sense of the World*, (Downers Grove, Illinois: IVP, 2012).

Marshall, Peter, *Mr Jones, Meet the Master*, (London: Fontana, 1980).

Matthews, Basil, *Livingstone, the Pathfinder*, (London: Livingstone Press, 1948).

Muggeridge, Malcolm, *Another King*, (Edinburgh: Saint Andrew Press, 1968).

Murray, John, *The Infallible Word*, (Westminster Theological Seminary, 1946).

Murray, John J., *Behind A Frowning Providence*, (Edinburgh: Banner of Truth, 1990).

Palmer, Benjamin Morgan, *Selected Writings*, (Edinburgh: Banner of Truth, 2014).

Peterson, Eugene, *The Message*, (Colorado Springs: Navpress, 1993).

Philip, James, *The Death and Resurrection of Christ* (unpublished).

Phillips, J. B., *The New Testament in Modern English*, (London: Geoffrey Bles, 1960).

Postman, Neil, *Amusing Ourselves to Death*, (New York: Penguin, 1985).

Randall, David J., *A Sad Departure*, (Edinburgh: Banner of Truth, 2015).

Randall, David J., [ed.], *Why we (still) believe*, (Fearn, Ross-shire: Christian Focus, 2017).

Robertson, David, *The Dawkins Letters*, (Fearn: Christian Focus, 2007).

Schaeffer, Francis, *The God who is there*, (Westmont, Illinois: InterVarsity Press, 1998).

Stewart, James S., *A Faith to Proclaim*, (London: Hodder & Stoughton, 1953).

Stott, John, *The Cross of Christ*, (London: IVP, 1986).

Stott, John, *Through the Bible Through the Year*, (Oxford: Lion Hudson, 2006).

*Strong's Exhaustive Concordance of the Bible*, (Nashville: Crusade Bible Publishers, 1890).

Taylor, Sir Thomas, *Where One Man Stands*, (Edinburgh: St Andrew Press, 1960).

Torrance, T. F., *Preaching Christ Today*, (Grand Rapids: Eerdmans, 1996).

Trueman, Karl, *The Wages of Spin*, (Fearn, Ross-shire: Christian Focus, 2004).

Watson, David C. K., *God's Freedom Fighters*, (Movement Books, 1972).

Waugh, Evelyn, *Brideshead Revisited*, (London: Penguin Books edition, 1960).

Whitehouse, Mary, *Quite Contrary*, (London: Pan Macmillan, 1993).

Wright, T., *Surprised by Scripture*, (London: SPCK, 2014).